FLYING
PAPER AIRPLANE
MODELS

Frank Ross, Jr.

ILLUSTRATED WITH
PHOTOGRAPHS AND DRAWINGS

Lothrop, Lee & Shepard Company • New York

This book is dedicated to DR. RALPH JUNKER
with warmest good wishes—ad astra cum Stampe!

Printed in the United States of America

2   3   4   5   79   78   77   76

Library of Congress Cataloging in Publication Data

Ross, Frank Xavier
    Flying paper airplane models.
    Bibliography: p.
    SUMMARY: Instructions for making and flying model airplanes
of today and of the future with information about the actual aircraft.
    1. Paper airplanes—Juvenile literature.
[1. Paper airplanes. 2. Handicraft. 3. Airplanes]
I. Title.
TL770.R67   629.133'1   74-22479
ISBN 0-688-41683-7
ISBN 0-688-51683-1 lib. bdg.

Other Books By Frank Ross, Jr.

HISTORIC PLANE MODELS
Their Stories and How to Make Them

MODEL SATELLITES AND SPACECRAFT
Their Stories and How to Make Them

JOBS IN MARINE SCIENCE

RACING CARS AND GREAT RACES

STORMS AND MAN

SPACE SCIENCE AND YOU

THE WORLD OF POWER AND ENERGY

THE WORLD OF MEDICINE

THE WORLD OF ENGINEERING

TRANSPORTATION OF TOMORROW

WEATHER
The Science of Meteorology from Ancient Times to the Space Ages

PARTNERS IN SCIENCE
A Survey of the International Geophysical Year

SUPERPOWER
The Story of Atomic Energy

YOUNG PEOPLE'S BOOK OF JET PROPULSION

Contents

McDonnell Douglas Corp.

Introduction

Making and flying paper airplanes has been a sport of boys and girls for many years. Today, this pleasure activity is probably more popular than ever. Even grown-ups are taking part in it.

There was once a more serious side to constructing paper airplane models. Late in the last century when many inventors were struggling to build a successful heavier-than-air flying machine, they sometimes tested their ideas with paper models. But the moment when the first practical airplane took to the sky has long since passed. Now making and flying paper airplane models is strictly a fun pastime. That is what this book is all about.

Most books that tell how to make paper planes use models that the authors themselves have designed. This book is different because the models in it are based on real aircraft. Brief descriptions of each of the planes used as models for the paper aircraft are included, and the book also has a list of words commonly used in the field of aeronautics.

Perhaps, after you have finished making the airplane models described in the pages ahead, you will also want to design your own. This is the real pleasure and thrill of airplane model making. Who knows?—you may even write a book about your creative activity, to share your enjoyment with fellow model makers.

Materials and Tools

Paper: Paper is the single most important material you will need to make your airplane models. The paper should not be too flexible, like the paper in your school notebook, or too rigid, like thin cardboard.

If the paper is too flexible, your model will not hold its shape and will be almost impossible to fly. On the other hand, if the paper is too rigid, the chances are your model will be too heavy. The moment you launch it, the model will dive instantly to the floor.

File folders are made of paper that is a good weight to use. You can probably find file folders or paper of similar weight in a craft supply shop, a five-and-dime store, or a well-stocked stationery store.

You may also use drawing paper to make your models. There are many kinds that are just about perfect for this purpose. Perhaps your art teacher will let you have a sheet or two to take home and experiment with. If you find that the paper works well, you can buy some at a craft or art supply store.

Glue: Almost all the paper models in this book have small parts that must be attached to the main sections. Glue will be necessary for this purpose. Elmer's Glue-All and Sobo are two very good adhesives. They dry fast, make strong attachments, and can barely be seen once they are dry. Equally important, these two glues will cause very little shrinkage in the paper. Both types of glue may be found at supermarkets, hardware stores, or stationery, craft, or art supply stores. Your models will not require too much gluing so buy the smallest bottle of glue available.

Tracing Paper: You may wish to transfer the patterns for the plane models to your construction paper freehand. Or you may decide to trace the patterns. In this case you will need tracing paper. Onionskin is normally used and you can probably buy it at an art or craft supply shop. You may also have some thin tissue paper at home that will do the job equally well.

If you trace, place the tracing paper over the pattern. Let the paper extend beyond the edge of the book page, so it can be taped to the table. Be sure to use a table with a smooth top such as Formica, plastic, or wood, so the tape will not damage it. Since most of the traced lines will be straight, use a ruler as a guide. Press lightly to avoid cutting through the paper with your pencil point. Trace all lines—solid and dotted.

When you have completed all the necessary tracing, remove the tracing paper from the pattern and turn it over. Place it on a large sheet of scrap paper and then, with a soft pencil, shade the entire back of the tracing paper. You can do this easily by holding the pencil at a shallow angle.

After the reverse side of the tracing paper is fully shaded, turn it right side up again. Place it, shaded side down, on the construction paper. Hold them together on the table with tape. It is important that the two sheets of paper do not move. Now go over the pattern on the tracing paper, once again using the ruler for all straight lines. The pencil shading will transfer the pattern to the construction paper as you draw. Only when you are certain that the entire pattern has been drawn should you remove the tracing paper.

Pencils: A soft black pencil will be needed for shading the back of your tracing paper. A medium pencil should be used for tracing the patterns and for transferring the patterns to the construction paper.

Ruler: In the course of making your paper plane models, you will find it necessary to do a great deal of measuring. A 12-inch ruler, clearly marked, will be needed. The ruler will also be used for drawing straight lines wherever these are called for on the patterns.

India Ink, Poster Paint, or Crayon: All the models have some markings or designs on them. Of course, you may omit them on your finished models if you wish. However, the markings and designs will make your models a good deal more realistic and attractive in appearance.

Although black ink, poster paint, or crayon are ordinarily used, it is not necessary for you to use that color. If you would prefer a bright color instead, such as red, green, or yellow, go ahead and use it. Many of the sport planes and commercial jetliners flying today have brightly colored markings. So there is no reason why your models should not be just as colorful.

One final suggestion: instead of using ink, paint, or crayon for marking your model, you might want to try Flair felt-tip pens. These are available in black as well as a variety of other colors. The pens are extremely easy to use and they make an effective finished design. Flair pens are

inexpensive and may be bought at a drugstore, art or craft
supply shop, or stationery store.

Drawing Pen or Paintbrush: If you decide to use India ink
for putting designs on your models, a drawing pen will be
needed. A paintbrush, of course, will be necessary if you
decide to paint the designs on your models instead.

Scissors: A sharp scissors is a must for constructing the paper
plane models described in this book. Try to use one that is
comfortable for your hand. This can be very important
when you are making difficult cuts—around curves, for
example.

Eraser: In transferring the patterns in the book to the paper
for your model, you may not always draw lines that satisfy
you the first time. In that case you will want to erase and
start over again. Use an eraser of art gum or a soap eraser.
These will not smear your pattern. Both kinds can be pur-
chased at an art supply shop or a stationery store.

Flying Your
Paper Airplane Models

After you have completed a paper airplane model, you will be anxious to fly it. Do not be too hasty about this. First make sure that all the parts you have glued to your model are firmly attached. Remember that your plane is made of paper and is therefore fragile. A good firm bump can transform your once beautiful model into a sad-looking wreck.

When you launch your flying paper plane, bear in mind that you are not throwing a baseball. It is not necessary to throw with all your strength. In fact, you must not do this, or your model will be unable to take to the air gracefully as it should. Instead, hold the model at the bottom center of the fuselage, or the tail end if this is the most convenient place (as in the supersonic models). Then, using an easy, gentle throwing motion, launch your model into the air.

If your model does not take to the air too well on the first launch, do not be discouraged. Builders of real airplanes often have the same problem during an initial test flight. Perhaps your model dives to the floor too quickly or curves to the right or left too sharply. There are things you can do to help matters.

If your model nose-dives too quickly, it is probably poorly balanced. It may be too heavy at the front end. Check this by balancing the model on your outstretched finger, placing your finger at the center point between nose and tail. If the model topples forward nose first, then you will know that it is out of balance. To correct this problem, attach a paper clip to the bottom edge of the fuselage slightly toward the tail of the plane. You may have to slide the paper clip along the fuselage until the model is properly balanced. Continue to experiment until you are completely satisfied.

If your paper model turns too sharply to the right or to the left, the fault could be a crooked vertical fin. Try bending the fin slightly to correct this problem. Bend the fin to the right if the model turns too sharply to the left, and bend to the left if it turns too sharply to the right.

Once you have become expert at launching your paper plane models, you may want to try putting them through more difficult maneuvers, like looping-the-loop. You might start with the supersonic models, because their wing shapes lend themselves well to different maneuvers.

Before sending the TU-144 or the Concorde paper model on a loop-the-loop journey, make certain that you cut the short sides of the wing flaps that are marked on the trailing edge of the wings. The flaps are the rectangular outlines. After cutting these as directed, you can bend them upward or downward, as though they were on hinges.

When you launch the Concorde paper model, bend the right and left wing flaps upward at a sharp angle. If it is a good flyer, the Concorde will describe a beautiful loop, then head for the floor on a long, graceful, gliding angle.

No doubt you will run into some difficulties as you try to

make your paper models fly. Experiment with bending the different parts of the models until the planes fly the way you want them to. After all, the models are only made of paper and changes on them can be made quickly and easily. You might even have to replace an entire wing or tail section. One of the real pleasures of flying paper airplane models, or plane models made of other materials, is to have them perform successfully because you have built in some ideas of your own. So if your models do not perform well, keep experimenting. Do not despair.

Flying paper airplane models by yourself can be fun, of course. But it is often more fun to do this with friends who also like to build model planes. As a group you can have contests to see whose model plane flies farthest, stays in the air longest, and is the best at making maneuvers.

A shared interest in airplane model making could lead to the formation of a club. Meeting at one another's homes at regular intervals, you could exchange information about different kinds of model airplanes to build and how best to make them.

The Boeing 707 Jetliner

The Boeing 707 jetliner was one of the earliest and most successful of the jet-powered airplanes designed for passenger service. The jetliner began its passenger-carrying career in August of 1958, and almost overnight it made obsolete the propeller-driven planes then in use. With smooth flying ability, long range, and a speed nearly twice that of the older planes, the 707 created a revolution in commercial flying. Within a few years it became a popular jetliner on airways throughout the world.

The Boeing 707-120 was the first model in the series of such aircraft. Later models are the 707-320 Intercontinental and the 707-320C. Improvements in the wing and body and more powerful jet engines allow the newer jetliners to fly farther and faster than the original models. The Intercontinental 707 can carry close to 190 passengers a distance of more than 6,000 miles at a speed of over 600 miles per hour.

The 707 is a big airplane even when it is compared to the jumbo jets now coming into service on the world's airlines. If

The Boeing 707 jetliner was one of the most successful of the early jet-powered passenger planes.

The Boeing Company

stood on its nose, the plane would be higher than a fourteen-story building. But despite its size, the plane's top speed is such that a World War II fighter plane—the fastest military plane in that war—would be unable to catch up with it.

Along with its great speed, the 707's ability to fly long distances makes it ideal for nonstop transoceanic air travel. Before this revolutionary jetliner came into service, the propeller-driven planes used on overseas air routes had to make one or more stops before spanning the oceans.

The Boeing 707-320C model was designed to serve as both a passenger-carrying jet airliner and an all-cargo carrier. The letter C distinguishes it from strictly passenger planes. The 707-320C has a stronger landing gear and cabin floor than other 707 models. The fuselage is equipped with an extra-wide door to allow easy loading and unloading of cargo. Special roller tracks are installed on the cabin floor so bulky cargo can be rolled into and out of the plane without too much effort. As an all-cargo plane, the 707-320C can airlift more than 91,000 pounds. When it is used to carry only passengers, the plane can be converted in a few hours to an all-passenger interior.

The 707 series of jetliners was a giant stride in improving air travel. The jet-powered airliner established new standards of comfort and speed difficult to surpass even with today's more advanced commercial aircraft.

PHYSICAL CHARACTERISTICS

Wingspan: 145 feet 9 inches.

Length: 152 feet 11 inches.

Height: 42 feet 5 inches.

Weight without cargo: 336,000 pounds.

Cargo capacity: Over 54,000 pounds as a passenger and cargo carrier; over 91,000 pounds as an all-cargo carrier.

Passenger capacity: Close to 190 with an economy seating arrangement.

Speed: More than 600 miles per hour.

Cruising altitude: 30,000 feet.

Range: More than 6,000 miles.

Engines: Four Pratt & Whitney JT3D turbofans producing 18,000 pounds of thrust each.

Crew: The 707 is operated by a flight crew of three.

Directions for Making the Boeing 707 Jetliner

Fuselage:

Trace and cut the pattern of the fuselage (Plate 1). Draw the design on both sides of the fuselage. Draw and cut the two slots as shown. The shorter one is for the horizontal tail fin; the longer one is for the wing.

Plate 1   707
FUSELAGE

Draw design on both sides of fuselage.

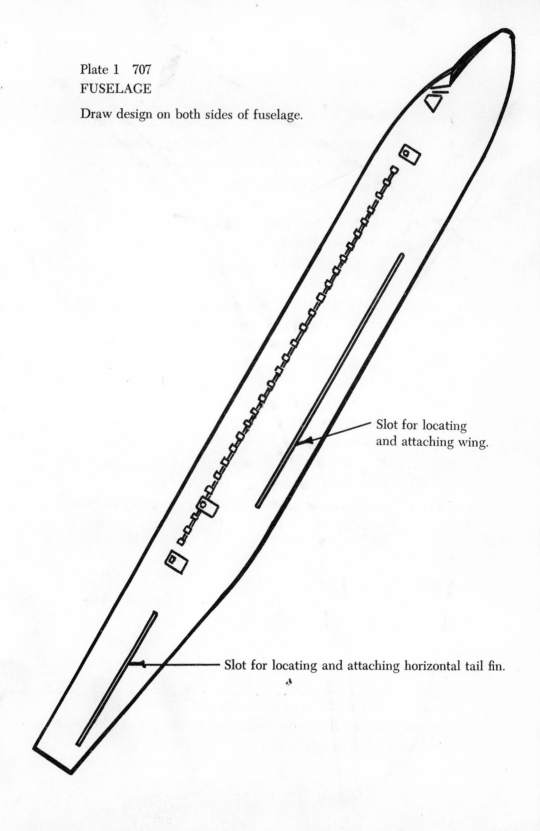

Slot for locating
and attaching wing.

Slot for locating and attaching horizontal tail fin.

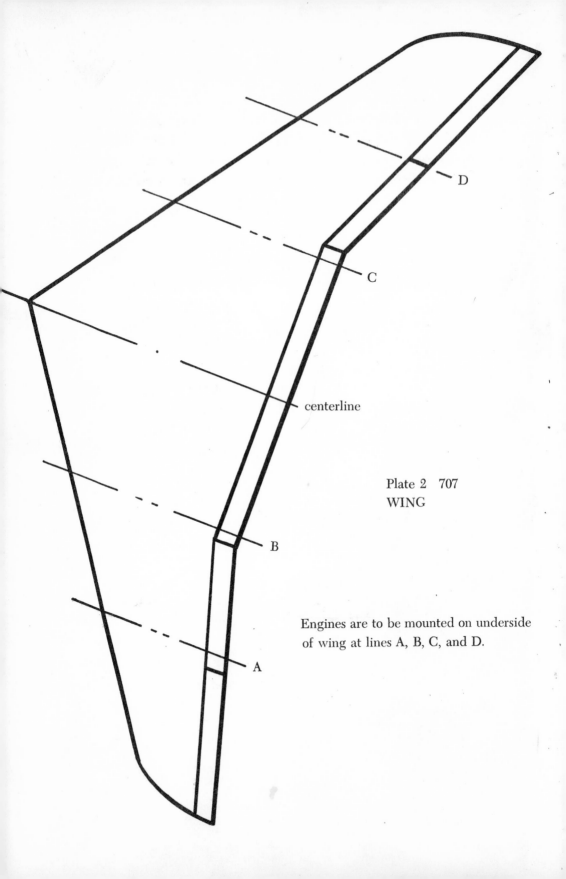

D

C

centerline

Plate 2   707
WING

B

Engines are to be mounted on underside
of wing at lines A, B, C, and D.

A

Wing:

Trace and cut the wing pattern (Plate 2). Draw the design on one side of the wing. Be sure to include the centerline, which is helpful when assembling the model. Also draw the lines that are labeled A, B, C, and D. These are needed for locating and attaching the engines.

Vertical Tail Fin:

Trace and cut the vertical tail fin (Plate 3). Do not omit the gluing tabs. Draw the design as indicated on both sides of the fin.

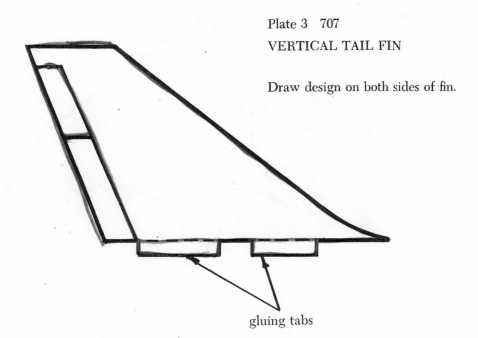

Plate 3   707

VERTICAL TAIL FIN

Draw design on both sides of fin.

gluing tabs

Horizontal Tail Fin:

Trace and cut the horizontal tail fin (Plate 4). Draw the design on one side. Include the centerline which is needed for attaching the fin to the fuselage.

Engines A and D, B and C:

Trace and cut the engine patterns (Plate 5), making two of each. Their only difference is in the length of the attachment portion.

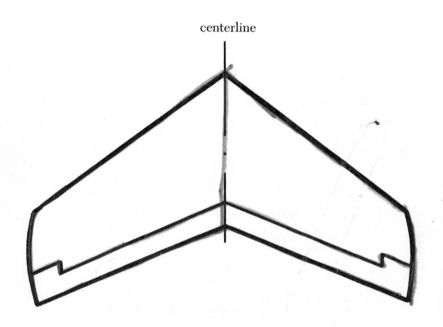

centerline

Plate 4   707   HORIZONTAL TAIL FIN

Glue only this part of attachment mount to the wing.

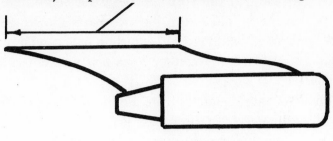

ENGINES A AND D

Make two.

Glue only this part of attachment mount to the wing.

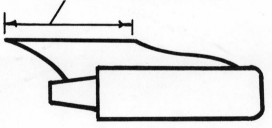

ENGINES B AND C

Make two.

Plate 5   707

ASSEMBLING THE 707 JETLINER

First attach the wing to the fuselage. Use the centerline of the wing as a guide to make sure the two parts are straight. Put several spots of glue along the centerline of the wing and hold the wing and fuselage together for a few moments until the glue hardens.

Next, attach the horizontal tail fin. Follow the same steps for doing this as for attaching the wing.

Now glue the engines to the underside of the wing. Use lines A, B, C, and D for locating and attaching the engines. You will find it easier to do this if you turn your model upside down. After putting glue on the attachment sections of the engines, hold each one in place for several moments until the glue hardens. Do not allow the engines to tilt to one side or the other.

Finally, glue the vertical tail fin to the tail end of the fuselage. Glue one tab to one side of the fuselage and the second tab to the other side. Try to mount the fin as straight as possible in relation to the fuselage. Your 707 will now be ready for commercial passenger service.

Model of the Boeing 707 jetliner.

The Boeing 727 Trijet

Many commercial jet planes flying today are of medium size, designed especially for providing air transportation on routes of up to 2,000 miles in length. One of the most popular of these aircraft, both in the United States and in countries throughout the world, is the Boeing 727 Trijet.

This plane is called the Trijet because it is powered by three jet engines. These are clustered toward the tail of the plane, giving it a distinctive appearance. As you can see in the photograph, there is one engine on either side of the body. The third engine is positioned on top of the body at the base of the vertical tail. The jet engines on the newer models of the 727 are designed to meet strict government regulations regarding noise and smoke pollution. The engines leave only a faint trace of smoke as compared with the dense streams that pour out of the older engines.

Although not comparable in size to the jumbo jets spanning oceans and continents with one leap, the 727 Trijet is not exactly a pygmy. It has a spacious interior. Large windows

The Boeing 727 Trijet airliner is a popular passenger plane on many medium-length air routes.   *The Boeing Company*

on either side of the body give passengers an excellent view of the airy world through which they are flying or of the land below. Each of the windows consists of three layers of material—two extra-strong glass layers and a plastic layer sandwiched between them. These triple-pane windows are especially designed to withstand the interior pressure of the plane's cabin while the aircraft is flying at an altitude of about six miles.

Probably the most unusual feature of the 727 Trijet is its horizontal tail structure. This is placed on top of the vertical fin to form a T-shape assembly. Like the main wings, the horizontal tail surfaces are swept backward to help the plane fly more efficiently at high speed. Another feature of the horizontal tail fin, not as easily seen, is its ability to move up and down. This allows the pilot to control the plane better at the low speeds needed for bringing the aircraft into an airport for a landing.

Increased ability to fly at low speeds has also been built into the aircraft's swept-back wings. These have a series of movable trailing-edge flaps and leading-edge flaps. The pilot uses these flaps for take-offs and landings.

Because the 727 Trijet can be effectively controlled at low speeds, it is especially well adapted for taking off and landing on short runways. This, of course, is the chief reason for the plane's existence and its use at medium-size airports.

PHYSICAL CHARACTERISTICS
Wingspan: 108 feet.
Length: 153 feet (overall).
Height: 34 feet (from tip of vertical fin to ground).
Weight without cargo: 191,000 pounds.
Cargo capacity: 21,000 pounds.
Passenger capacity: 122 to 189.
Speed: 570 to 605 miles per hour.
Cruising altitude: 30,000 to 40,000 feet.
Range: 1,500 to 2,500 miles.
Engines: Three Pratt & Whitney jet engines, ranging in thrust from 14,500 pounds to 15,500 pounds.
Crew: The 727 is operated by a flight crew of three.

Directions for Making the Boeing 727 Trijet

Fuselage:
Trace and cut the pattern for the fuselage (Plate 6). Draw the windows on both sides of the body. Also draw the design on the nose section and the cockpit windows. Draw and cut the slot in the lower part of the body. The wing slides into the slot. The slot is to be slightly longer than the widest part of the wing; this is because the wing may have to be adjusted forward or backward to give the model the best possible balance for flying.

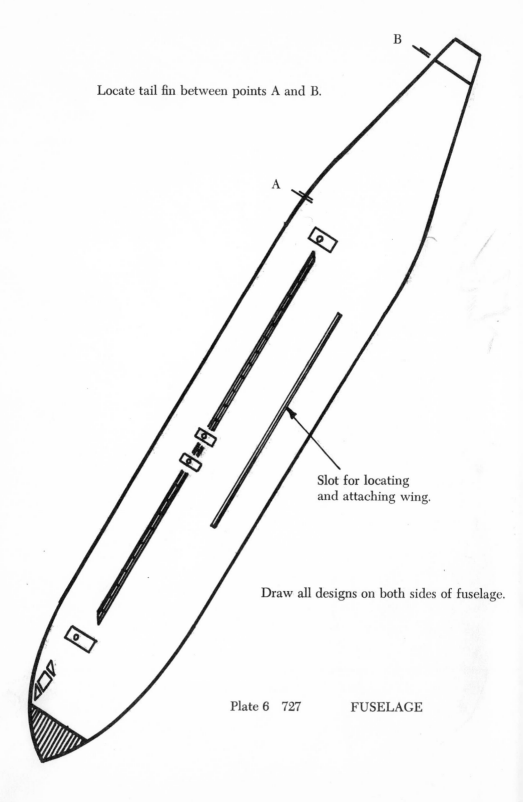

Locate tail fin between points A and B.

B

A

Slot for locating
and attaching wing.

Draw all designs on both sides of fuselage.

Plate 6   727   FUSELAGE

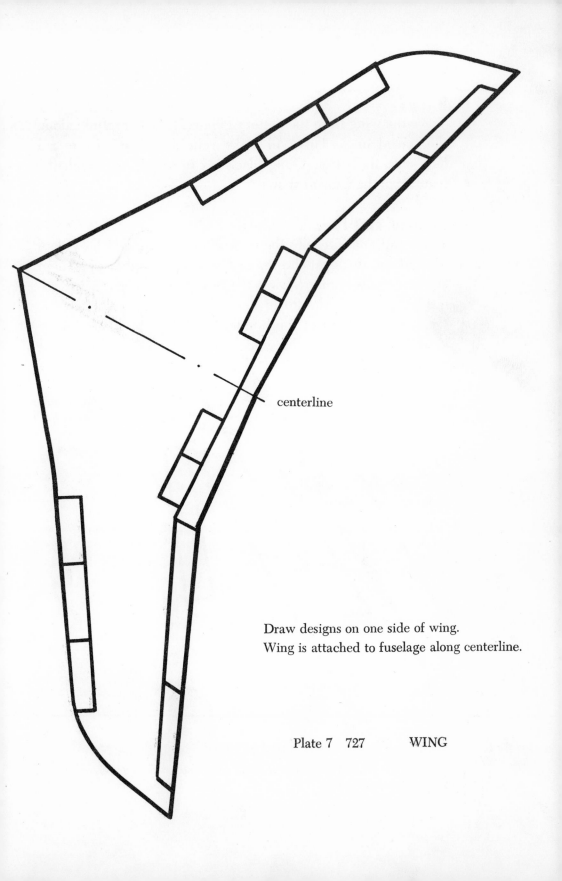

centerline

Draw designs on one side of wing.
Wing is attached to fuselage along centerline.

Plate 7   727   WING

Wing:

Trace the wing from the pattern (Plate 7). Cut carefully along the traced lines. This will make your model attractive and help it to fly better. Using black ink or crayon, draw all the features of the wing as shown.

Vertical Tail Fin:

Trace and cut carefully the outline for the vertical fin (Plate 8). Cut the slot near the top of the fin. Remember that there are two small gluing tabs at the bottom of the fin. They are needed to attach the fin to the tail end of the plane's body. Draw the features on both sides of the fin in black ink or crayon. Also draw in the guide line for attaching the tail fin engine.

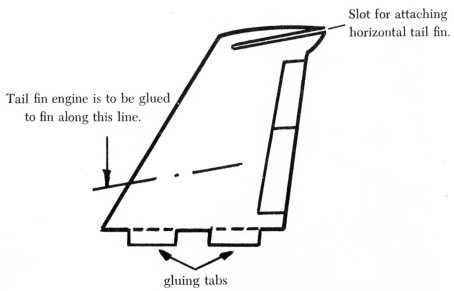

Slot for attaching horizontal tail fin.

Tail fin engine is to be glued to fin along this line.

gluing tabs

Glue tabs to opposite sides of plane's body.

Plate 8   727   VERTICAL TAIL FIN

Draw design along rear edge of fin on both sides.

Horizontal Tail Fin:

Trace and cut the horizontal tail fin (Plate 9). Again, try to make your cuts as neat as possible to help give the model an attractive appearance. Draw the designs on one side of the fin in black ink or crayon. Also draw in the centerline.

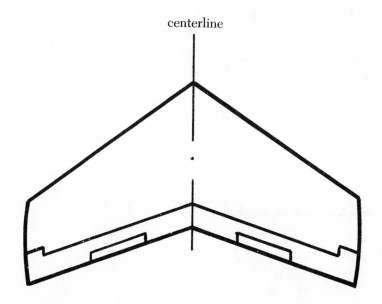

centerline

Draw design along rear edge of fin. Fin is to be attached to top of vertical fin along centerline.

Plate 9   727   HORIZONTAL TAIL FIN

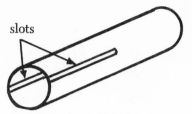

slots

Cut two slots in cylinder as shown.
They are used to glue engine
to vertical tail fin.

TAIL FIN ENGINE
Make one engine from the flat pattern above. Roll to the
approximate size shown at right. Overlap edges to dotted line
and glue.

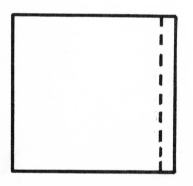

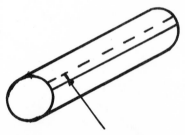

Overlap edges to dotted line and glue.

SIDE ENGINE
Make two.
Engines are made from flat pattern above. Roll paper into
cylinders—approximate size shown at right.

Bend gluing tabs
along dotted lines.

gluing tab —

gluing tab —

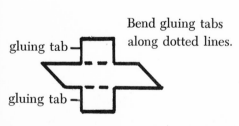

ENGINE STRUT
Make two.

Attach strut to engine as shown.

Glue one tab to the engine. Glue second tab
to side of plane. See photo for proper placement.

Plate 10   727

Engines:

The three engines of the Trijet are simply rectangular pieces that are rolled into cylinders and glued at the edges. Trace and cut the engine patterns (Plate 10). Select a lighter weight paper for the engines than that used for the body and wings. If the paper for the engines is too heavy, it will throw the whole plane out of balance and this will cause problems when you try to make the model fly. It may help to roll the paper if you do it over a thick pencil. The tail fin engine has two slots cut into it. These are needed for attaching the engine to the vertical tail fin. See Plate 10 for the size and placement of the slots.

Engine Struts:

Use paper of the same weight as that for the model's body and wings. Trace and cut the two engine struts or attachments (Plate 10). Bend the gluing tabs on the two long sides of each attachment along the dotted lines as shown. Make both bends in the same direction so that when the piece is looked at from the end it has a U shape.

ASSEMBLING THE 727 TRIJET

Start assembling the Trijet by sliding the wing through the slot you have cut in the body of the plane. The centerline of the wing should be exactly in line with the fuselage. Do not glue the wing yet.

Next, assemble the horizontal and vertical tail fins. Slide the horizontal fin into the slot cut in the top of the vertical fin. Put a slight dab of glue along the centerline on the top and bottom of the horizontal fin where it will slide into the slot. The two sections must be firmly joined.

After the two tail sections are firmly glued together, attach the whole assembly to the tail section of the body. Place it in position between points A and B as shown on Plate 6. Use the gluing tabs on the bottom of the vertical fin for attaching it to the body of the plane. Glue one tab on one side of the body; bend and glue the other tab on the opposite side.

Next, glue the Trijet's three engines in place. Start with the tail fin engine. Put a small amount of glue in the slots so that when the engine is pushed onto the vertical fin it will stay firmly in place.

Glue one of the engine struts to each of the other two engines. After the struts have become fixed, use the other gluing tab of each strut to attach the engines to the body. Make sure that the side engines are placed directly under the tail fin engine.

Now try to balance the model on your extended index finger. You may have to move the wing forward or backward in its slot, or even side to side, to find the right position to make the model balance. When you have found the correct position, glue the wing in place. When it has become firmly glued, the Trijet will be ready for its first test flight.

Good luck! And happy landing!

Model of the Boeing 727 Trijet.

The McDonnell Douglas DC-10

The McDonnell Douglas DC-10 trijet is another of the giant jet air transports that have brought increased luxury and comfort to air travelers the world over.

The DC-10 is a versatile airplane that can be changed quickly to perform a number of different transport jobs. Its main role is as a luxury airliner flying on national and international air routes. It can be transformed into a jumbo jet carrying up to 345 passengers in economy class or it can be changed into a combination airliner with its cabin divided into first class and tourist class seatings. And finally, the DC-10 can be altered to become an all-cargo carrier. When changed into a cargo model, the DC-10 is identified as the DC-10F, the F indicating freight.

The DC-10 jetliner is the tenth in a series of commercial air transports carrying the name Douglas that have been built without interruption for more than thirty-eight years. The early models carried the name Douglas only, after the man who designed and built them, Donald Douglas. He was one of the most famous of the pioneer airplane designers and builders in the United States. Eventually the Douglas Company joined forces with the McDonnell Aircraft Corporation, an outstanding builder of military aircraft, to form the McDonnell Douglas Company.

The first completed DC-10 took to the skies on August 29, 1970, on a maiden flight that lasted for almost three and a half hours. It proved extremely successful, and a little less than a year later the big jetliner was put into commercial service by American Airlines on its Chicago-Los Angeles route. The DC-10 began transcontinental air service on August 14, 1971, when United Airlines began using the giant jet on its air route between San Francisco and Washington, D.C.

Although the DC-10's jet engines are the most advanced and powerful in existence—40,000 to 50,000 pounds of thrust—they are almost completely smokeless as compared to older engine types. Also important for people living near commercial airports, these jet engines produce a noise level that is not unbearable. The engines meet all the regulations of the Federal government with respect to noise and pollution.

The roomlike interior of the DC-10 is almost 19 feet wide

The McDonnell Douglas DC-10 is one of the new breed of wide-bodied jetliners.   *McDonnell Douglas Corp.*

The giant size of the DC-10 is clearly shown by comparison with the men working beneath it. *McDonnell Douglas Corp.*

and 8 feet high. Because of its great width, the cabin has two aisles running its length. The cabin has eight doors for use in case of emergency when passengers must leave the aircraft in a hurry. Six of the doors are wide enough so that two people can pass through side by side.

The DC-10 is normally operated by a flight crew of three, using the most advanced navigation equipment. The crew can bring the DC-10 to a safe landing even when visibility conditions at an airport are near zero.

PHYSICAL CHARACTERISTICS

Wingspan: 155 feet 4 inches (for international flying, the DC-10's wingspan is 161 feet 4 inches).

Length: 181 feet 5 inches.

Height: 58 feet 1 inch.

Weight without cargo: 261,500 pounds.

Cargo capacity: 100,336 pounds.

Passenger capacity: 230 to 380.

Speed: More than 600 miles per hour.

Cruising altitude: 30,000 feet.

Range: 4,400 miles for the domestic flying model; 6,100 miles for the DC-10 used on international routes.

Engines: Three jet engines—either General Electric or Pratt & Whitney—with a thrust output of 40,000 to 50,000 pounds.

Crew: The DC-10 is operated by a crew of three.

Directions for Making the McDonnell Douglas DC-10

Fuselage:

Trace and cut out the fuselage as shown in the pattern (Plate 11). Draw the designs as shown on both sides of the fuselage. Draw the slot near the tail end of the fuselage, and cut it through. This will be needed for attaching the horizontal tail fin.

Wing:

Trace and cut out the wing as shown on the drawing (Plate 12). Draw the various markings on the upper side of the wing only. Do not omit the centerline. This is necessary for gluing the body to the wing. Cut the short sides of the two large flaps as indicated. These flaps can be bent up or down to make your model more maneuverable.

Horizontal Tail Fin:

Trace and cut out the horizontal tail fin as shown in the pattern (Plate 13). Include the centerline in your drawing. This will be helpful when you attach the tail to the body. Draw the flaps along the rear edge of the fin.

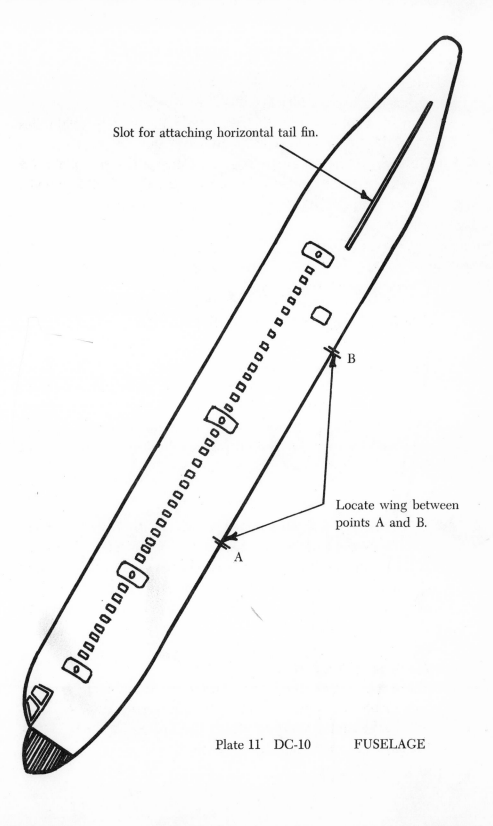

Slot for attaching horizontal tail fin.

B

Locate wing between
points A and B.

A

Plate 11   DC-10   FUSELAGE

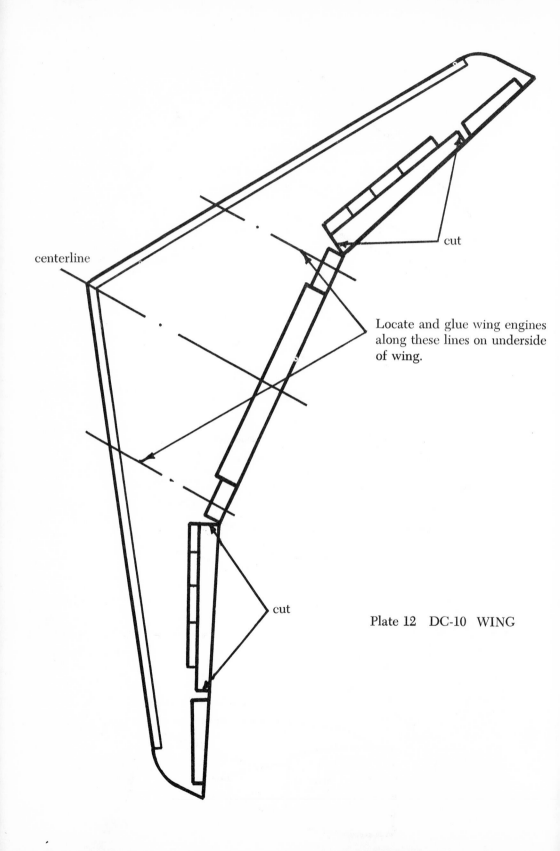

centerline

cut

Locate and glue wing engines
along these lines on underside
of wing.

cut

Plate 12   DC-10   WING

centerline

HORIZONTAL TAIL FIN

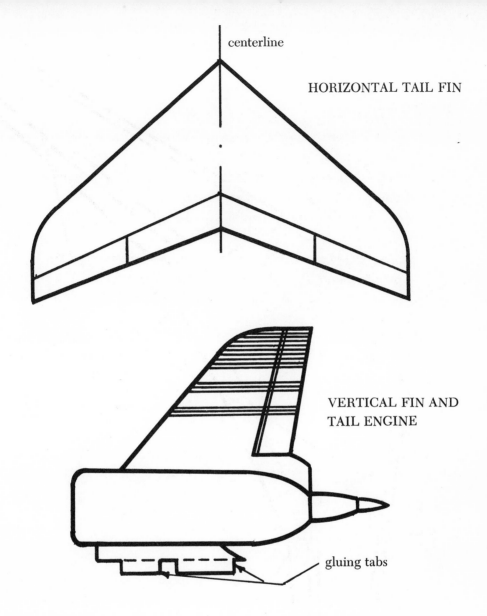

VERTICAL FIN AND
TAIL ENGINE

gluing tabs

Plate 13   DC-10

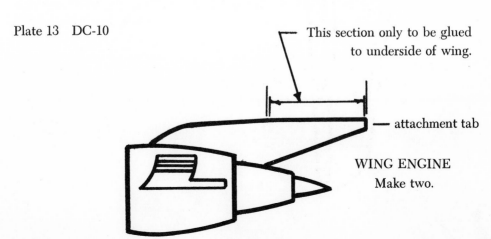

This section only to be glued
to underside of wing.

attachment tab

WING ENGINE
Make two.

Vertical Fin and Tail Engine:

Trace and cut the combination vertical fin and tail engine as shown on the drawing (Plate 13). Include the gluing tabs. They are needed for attaching the fin to the body of the plane. Draw the design on both sides of the fin. Use black ink or crayon for this, or use a color if you prefer.

Wing Engines:

Use the same kind of paper that you have used for making the rest of the plane. Trace and cut two wing engines as shown on the pattern (Plate 13). Draw the design on both sides of each engine. Do not omit the attachment tab on the top of the engine. This is needed to glue the engines to the under-side of the wings.

ASSEMBLING THE DC-10

Start putting your paper model together by gluing the wing and body together. Place a few spots of glue along the center-line of the wing. Press the lower edge of the plane's body onto the glue, making sure to place the wing between points A and B on the fuselage. Hold the body upright and steady for a few moments until the glue hardens. Do not permit it to tilt to one side or the other. This would spoil the flying ability of your model as well as detract from its appearance.

Next, attach the horizontal tail fin to the body. Place several spots of glue along the centerline of the fin. Slide the fin through the slot cut into the tail end of the body. When the centerline and edge of the body are exactly straight in relation to one another, press the two sections together. Hold the fin in place for a few moments until the glue hardens.

Now glue the vertical fin and tail engine to the fuselage using the gluing tabs. Position the fin on the body as shown in the photo and hold it in place until the glue hardens.

Finally, glue the two wing engines in place. Put a generous amount of glue along the top edge of the attachment tab. Press this against the lower side of the wing in the position where the engine is to be glued. Check the wing pattern (Plate 12) for the exact location. Hold the engine in place for a few moments until the glue hardens. Do not let the engines lean to either side, as this would take away from the neat appearance of your model.

Your flying paper model of the DC-10 is now complete and ready to go into flying service!

Model of the McDonnell Douglas DC-10.

The Cessna 150-Aerobat

Flying one's own airplane has become a popular sport. The thrill of leaving the earth and swooping and gliding through the sky has caught the enthusiasm of large numbers of young men and women. Every weekend when the weather permits, countless numbers of small airports throughout the country are alive with activity as youthful pilots take their small planes aloft for a spin. Often they just fly near the airport, improving their skill at landings and take-offs. Sometimes they are more adventurous and, either alone or with several other sports flyers, they make a short hop to another private airfield a hundred or so miles away.

The aircraft that sports flyers take aloft are of endless variety and colors. A growing number are old-time planes that young sports flyers have rebuilt and made flyable again, just the way sports car lovers have rebuilt old automobiles. A few are planes that have been built from kits. But the majority are modern airplanes bought from manufacturers of private air-

The Cessna Aerobat is a favorite aircraft of many who love to fly for sport. *Cessna Aircraft Company*

craft. One of these has proved to be not only a great flying machine but extremely attractive to look at. It is the Cessna 150-Aerobat.

The Aerobat is a high-wing monoplane that, in addition to being popular for private flying, can also be used as a training plane and, for the skilled flyer, as an aircraft to do aerobatics. The special models of the Aerobat for aerobatic flying are built extra strong. For loops and dives, the aircraft must be exceptionally sturdy to withstand the greater stresses and strains. To distinguish this model from others in its class, a checkerboard pattern is painted on the vertical fin.

For training purposes an aircraft must be extremely sensitive to control and must all but fly itself. The Aerobat meets those needs and more. Its designers have built certain features into the plane with an instructor and student flyer in mind. For example, the cabin is well insulated so the instructor and student can talk to one another without shouting over the roar of the engine. And it is roomy, giving the instructor freedom of movement to demonstrate certain actions to the student when necessary.

Instruments—bank-and-turn indicator, altimeter, and speedometer, among others—are vital to all aircraft. On the Aerobat these have been designed and arranged in such a way that the student, or the seasoned pilot, can see instantly what they are indicating. It is absolutely essential for the flyer to know how his airplane is behaving at all times.

The Aerobat and its sister models all have a tri-cycle landing gear. That is, the plane has a nose wheel and two wheels on either side of the cabin. This type of landing gear helps to make landings and take-offs easier. Also, it makes the plane level when it is on the ground, which is more comfortable for the occupants. On the paper model Aerobat, this landing gear is eliminated. It would only interfere with the model's flying ability.

PHYSICAL CHARACTERISTICS
Wingspan: 32 feet 8½ inches.
Length: 23 feet 9 inches.
Height: 8 feet (from top edge of vertical fin to ground).
Weight without cargo: 1,600 pounds.
Cargo capacity: 600 pounds.
Passenger capacity: 3.
Top speed: 122 miles per hour.
Cruising speed: 117 miles per hour.
Maximum flying altitude: 12,600 feet.
Cruising altitude: 7,000 feet.
Range: 880 miles.
Engines: One O-200A engine.

Directions for Making
the Cessna 150-Aerobat

Fuselage:

Trace and cut out the fuselage as shown in the drawing (Plate 14). Make sure that the vertical fin is included. This fin and the fuselage are one piece. Draw the design on the body and vertical fin on both sides. Notice that the fin has a checkerboard pattern, which indicates that this particular model has been designed especially for aerobatics. Use black ink or crayon, or any other color you wish, to draw the design. Try to make your design as neat as possible. This will add to the attractiveness of your finished model. Cut the slot in the tail end of the body for the horizontal fin.

Wing:

Trace and cut the Aerobat's wing carefully, using the pattern (Plate 15). Draw the design on the top side of the wing with black ink or crayon, or any color you choose. Draw this design very carefully so your model will look attractive when finished.

Horizontal Fin:

Trace and cut the horizontal fin as shown in the drawing (Plate 16). Draw the design on the top side of the fin only. Use the same colors that you used for the design on the top of the wing.

Wing Struts:

Trace and cut two struts as shown in the drawing (Plate 16). Bend the ends of the struts at the dotted lines.

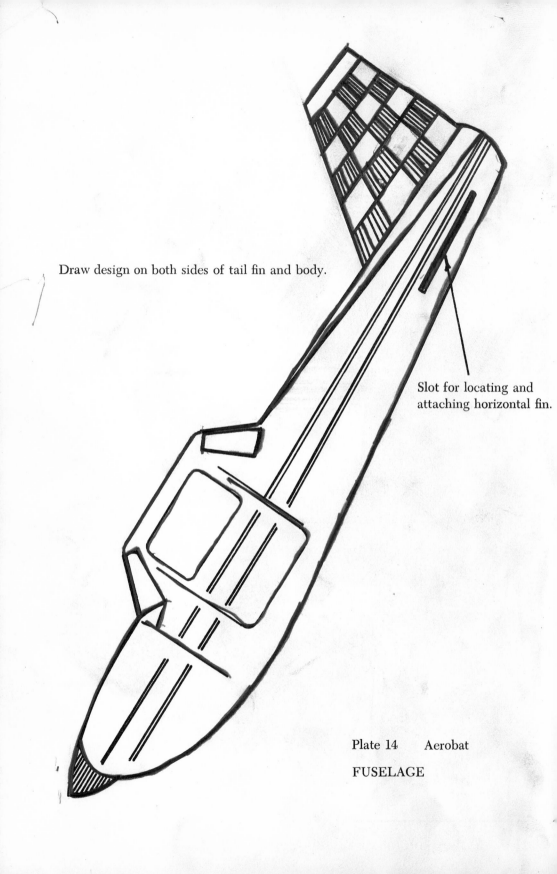

Draw design on both sides of tail fin and body.

Slot for locating and
attaching horizontal fin.

Plate 14   Aerobat

FUSELAGE

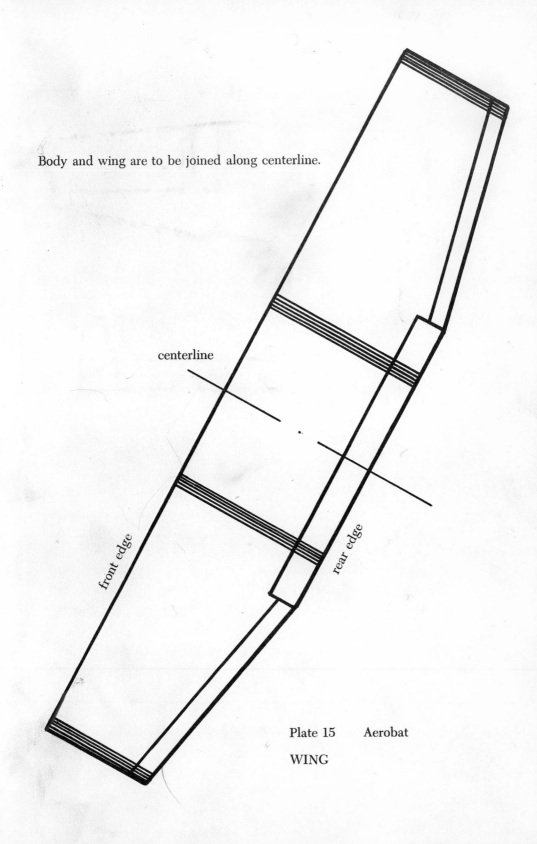

Body and wing are to be joined along centerline.

centerline

front edge

rear edge

Plate 15   Aerobat

WING

Plate 16   Aerobat

Horizontal fin and body
are to be joined along centerline.

centerline

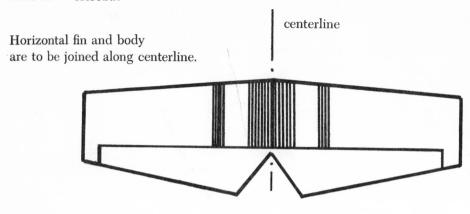

HORIZONTAL FIN

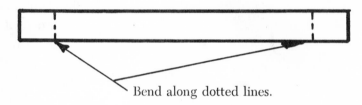

Bend along dotted lines.

WING STRUT
Make two.

ASSEMBLING THE AEROBAT

Start putting your Aerobat paper model together by attaching the wing to the body. Place a small amount of glue along the dotted centerline on the underside of the wing. Glue the wing carefully to the top edge of the Aerobat's cabin. You may find it easier to do this if you turn the wing and body of the plane upside down. Be patient. Keep holding the two sections together until the glue has made a firm attachment.

After the wing has been permanently fixed to the body, attach the horizontal fin. This is inserted through the slot cut in the tail end of the body. Again, put a small amount of glue along the dotted centerline of the fin, on the underside. Hold the fin in place for a few moments until the glue hardens.

To finish putting your paper model of the Aerobat together, attach the two wing struts. When you glue these in position, make sure that the bent ends attached to the body point downward, and the bent ends attached to the wing point outward toward the tips of the wing. Both struts, when firmly fixed, will help to give rigidity to the wing as well as some resemblance to the real plane.

Do not try to fly your Aerobat model immediately after putting the struts in place. Give the glue a chance to dry and make a tight bond on all the parts. On the first couple of launchings your plane will undoubtedly make some hard landings, and even the mildest bump can cause parts that are not well glued to come undone. Be patient and you will become an expert flyer!

Model of the Cessna 150-Aerobat.

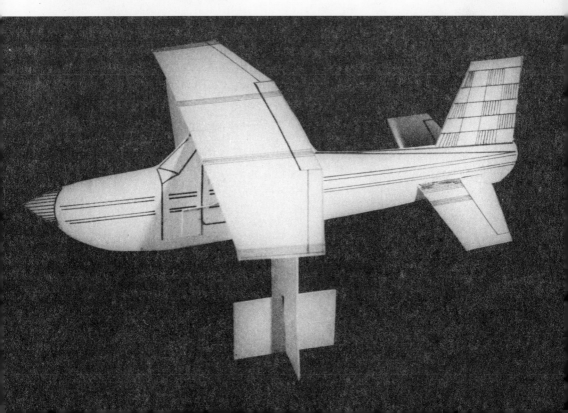

The Boeing 747 Jumbo Jet Airliner

Small planes, medium-size planes, large planes—all play an important role in the business of running commercial airlines. Small planes are used on short air routes for the local transport of passengers. Medium-size planes are commonly flown on intercity air routes, traveling as much as 1,500 miles. The giant air transports span oceans and entire continents. These are the pride of the commercial air fleets. They are the swift couriers, bearing passengers and cargo, that help to bind our world into a single family of nations.

The Boeing 747 jumbo jet airliner is the most spectacular of the big planes currently flying on the world's air routes. It is the largest airplane ever designed for carrying passengers and cargo, measuring just over 231 feet from nose to tail. The tip of the monster jet's tail is more than 63 feet above the ground, higher than a five-story building. The main cabin is 20 feet wide with two aisles running lengthwise instead of one as on smaller planes. When the cabin is filled to near capacity with almost 400 passengers, the 747 looks like a small theater in flight.

The Boeing 747 jumbo jetliner is the largest commercial plane in service on the air routes of the world. *The Boeing Company*

Above the main cabin at the front of the huge plane is the flight deck. Here are the scores of instruments and controls operated by the pilot, copilot, and flight engineer as they guide this aerial giant through the skies. Directly in back of the flight deck is a small lounge area. Passengers who wish to stretch their legs during a long flight can reach the lounge by climbing a short, spiral staircase. Refreshments are served in the lounge. People who have flown aboard the 747 say it is an absolutely revolutionary experience in air travel. The aircraft's interior is so spacious that it is difficult to realize one is inside an airplane thousands of feet above the earth.

The 747 is driven through the skies by four of the most powerful jet engines made in the United States. One of these engines alone has more than twice the power of the engines used on earlier commercial jet planes. The engines are mounted on the underside of the wings, two on each side of the fuselage.

Because such a large number of passengers can be carried by the 747 superjet, its designers had to give special attention to the best means for entering and leaving the plane. This consideration is especially important in case of emergencies. The designers placed ten doorways in the mammoth cabin, five on each side. Only in an emergency when passengers have to leave the plane quickly are all ten exits used. Normally, only a few of the doors are used by the passengers for boarding and disembarking, while others are used for servicing the giant plane.

Getting several hundred people out of an airplane as hurriedly as possible in an emergency is no small achievement. The 747 jumbo jet is equipped with rubberized chutes. When needed, they are quickly inflated and attached to the exits. Passengers simply slide down the chutes, just as children do on playground slides.

When the 747 operates at full capacity with passengers and cargo, it tips the scales at about 350 tons. To bring this enormous weight to earth safely and gently, the monster plane has an enormously strong landing gear. The main portion directly under the wings consists of four units of four wheels each. Thus, there are sixteen wheels in all at this point that take the full impact of the plane at the moment of touchdown on the runway. The nose gear has two wheels. The entire landing gear of the 747 has been designed to take the weight of the giant plane evenly when it comes to earth. If this were not the case, the plane as well as the airport's runway would be damaged.

The first completed 747 superjet took to the skies on February 9, 1969. About a year later, on January 20, 1970, Pan American World Airways put the first of the giant jets into regular commercial service between New York and London. Now this huge aircraft is in regular operation with all the major airlines throughout the world.

Since the first 747 carrying only passengers came into airline service, several other models have been built for special airline needs. One is strictly a freighter model and is designated the 747F. The F stands for freight. This model has a hinged nose section that swings upward. When the entire front end of the plane is open, cargo can be put aboard and removed easily. To help load and unload cargo, the interior of the freighter has been equipped with a special mechanical handling system. Cargo containers can be rolled into and out of the plane quickly with little difficulty. Three men can load and unload the 747F in less than an hour.

The 747F can airlift 125 tons of cargo for a maximum distance of nearly 3,000 miles. It can carry a smaller load of 100 tons for a distance of almost 4,000 miles. This means the giant jet can easily leap-frog the Atlantic Ocean with any kind of cargo that has to be delivered quickly. One of the 747 test models leading to the creation of the 747F lifted a record load of 826,700 pounds—more than 400 tons.

Another of the newer models of the 747 superjet is the 747C. This plane has a dual nature. It can be changed in a very short time to carry passengers or cargo. Hence the initial C which stands for convertible. Some airlines like to have this kind of aircraft in their fleet so they can meet the special needs of their transport business in the most efficient way possible. At some times of the year, cargo-carrying needs may be greater, while at other times there may be a greater need for carrying passengers. In either case the 747C allows the airline to adapt the jumbo jet to whatever the business demands.

The 747 superjet and all the different models in that family of aircraft have been designed and built by one of the oldest airplane manufacturers in the United States, the Boeing Company. Its designers and engineers have been building military and commercial aircraft since the early decades of this century. The graceful 747 superjet is the supreme technical achievement of this experienced builder of airplanes.

PHYSICAL CHARACTERISTICS

Wingspan: 195 feet 9 inches.

Length: 231 feet 4 inches.

Height: 63 feet 6 inches (from tip of vertical tail to ground).

Fuselage width: 21 feet 5 inches.

Weight without cargo: 353,398 pounds.

Cargo capacity: 103,170 pounds.

Passenger capacity: 374 to 500.

Speed: 600 miles per hour.

Cruising altitude: 30,000 feet plus.

Range: More than 5,000 miles.

Engines: Four turbofan Pratt & Whitney jet engines with up to 47,000 pounds of thrust each.

Crew: The 747 is operated by a flight crew of three.

Directions for Making the Boeing 747 Jumbo Jet

Fuselage:

Trace and cut the fuselage, following the pattern (Plate 17). Using black ink or crayon, or any other color you may choose, draw the design on both sides of the fuselage. Cut a slot to the size shown on the pattern in the tail end of the fuselage. This is needed for attaching the horizontal tail fin. Also cut the slot in the fuselage for the main wing.

Wing:

Trace and cut the wing as shown on the pattern (Plate 18). Do this carefully, since it will help the model to fly better and will make it more attractive in appearance. Draw the design on one side of the wing. Also draw the centerline.

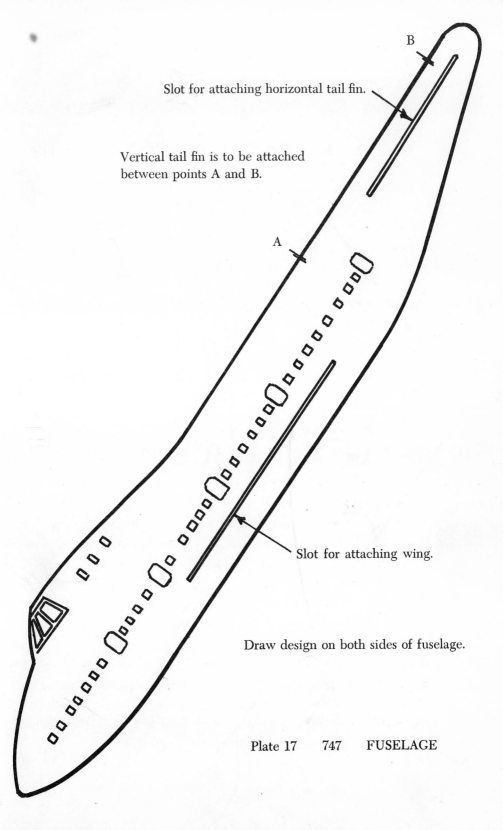

Slot for attaching horizontal tail fin.

Vertical tail fin is to be attached
between points A and B.

Slot for attaching wing.

Draw design on both sides of fuselage.

Plate 17   747   FUSELAGE

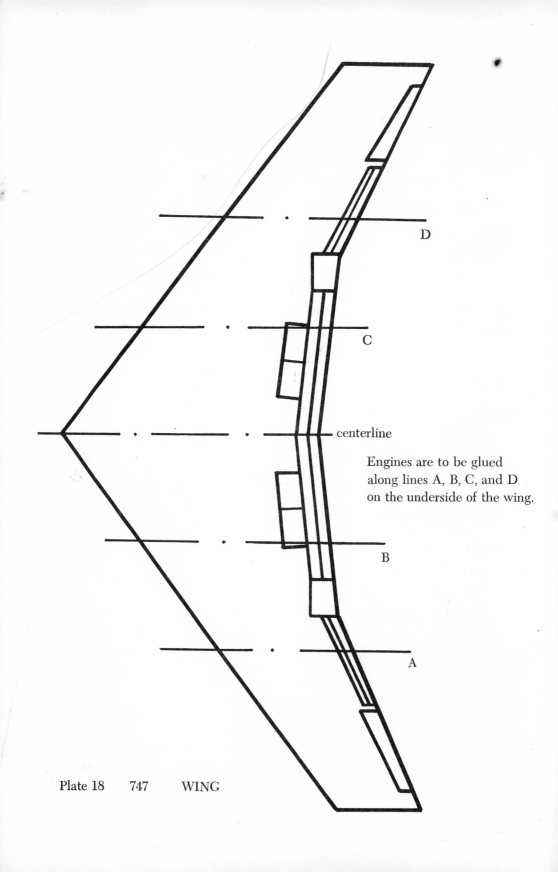

D

C

centerline

Engines are to be glued
along lines A, B, C, and D
on the underside of the wing.

B

A

Plate 18   747   WING

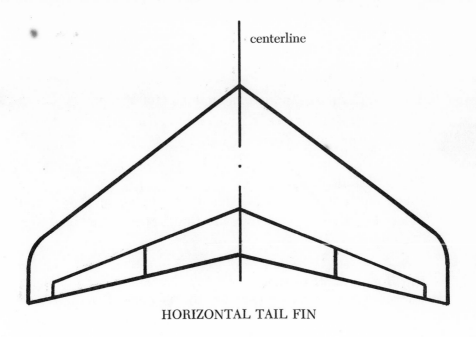

centerline

HORIZONTAL TAIL FIN

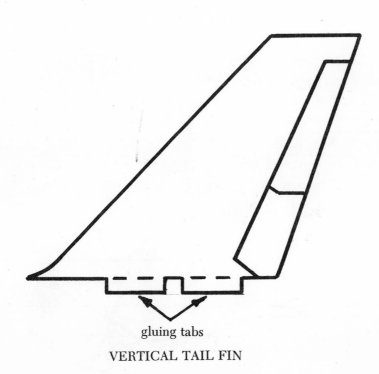

gluing tabs

VERTICAL TAIL FIN

Plate 19   747

Horizontal Tail Fin:

Trace and cut the horizontal tail fin, following the pattern (Plate 19). Draw the centerline on the fin as shown, and draw the design on both sides of the fin.

Vertical Tail Fin:

Trace and cut the vertical tail fin as shown in the pattern (Plate 19). Be sure to include the gluing tabs. Draw the design on both sides of the fin.

Engines and Mounts:

Use a lighter weight paper for the engines than that used for the rest of the model. The engines on this model are flat, two-dimensional pieces. Each engine and the mount for gluing it to the wing are made from one piece. Trace and cut four of these as shown in the pattern (Plate 20). Draw the design on each engine very carefully on both sides.

ASSEMBLING THE 747

Put several spots of glue along the centerline of the wing. Allow these to dry for a few moments until the glue becomes tacky. Then slide the wing through the slot of the fuselage.

This portion of mount is to be glued to underside of wing. Point A is to be at front edge of wing.

Plate 20   747

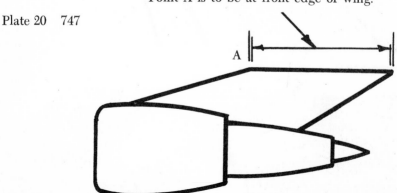

ENGINE AND MOUNT
Make four.

Be sure the slot and the centerline of the wing are lined up exactly straight. Hold the two sections together firmly for a few moments until the glue hardens.

Next glue the horizontal tail fin to the fuselage. Slide the fin through the slot in the tail section after putting several spots of glue along the centerline of the fin. Hold the fin in place for a few moments until the glue hardens.

To attach the vertical fin to the tail end of the fuselage, glue one of the gluing tabs on either side of the fuselage and hold the fin in place for a few moments while the glue hardens. Be sure to position the vertical fin between points A and B on the fuselage. The photo of the model shows the correct position.

Gluing the engines to the wing is the last step in assembling your flying model. Put glue along the top edge of the engine mounts, then press and hold against the underside of the wing. It may be best to do this with the model in an upside down position. Lines A, B, C, and D on the wing pattern show the correct location for the engines. Your model of the 747 is now complete and ready to be flown.

Model of the Boeing 747 jumbo jet.

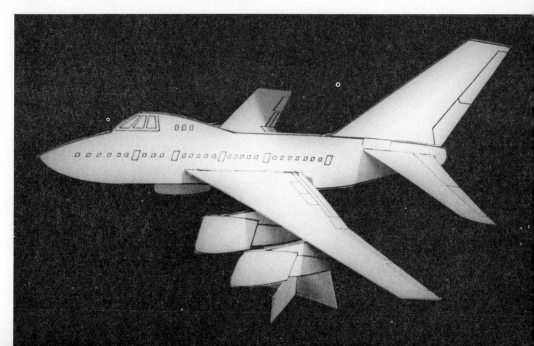

The L-1011 Tristar Jetliner

Operators of airlines must not only be concerned with the day-to-day running of their transport service; they also have to look to the years ahead. They must consider what the demands on their service will be a decade or more in the future and then plan to meet those demands. These future plans are centered almost wholly on new types of aircraft—planes that can carry more people, more comfortably, farther, faster, and at a more economical cost. Several of these new kinds of airplanes are already in existence and flying, including the outstanding L-1011 Tristar jetliner.

The Tristar is one of the new breed of aircraft known as a wide-bodied jet. Its cabin interior is almost 20 feet in width, nearly double that of the older airliners. Although it is powered by only three jet engines, which give the L-1011 its name, Tristar, it is capable of carrying up to 400 passengers and can bear this human cargo more than 3,000 miles.

The flying abilities of the Tristar are made possible by the aircraft's massive, powerful turbojet engines. Their 40,000 to

The L-1011 is one of the new wide-bodied jets now flying on the world's airways.   *Lockheed-California Company*

50,000 pounds of thrust make them more than twice as powerful as the engines on the older commercial jetliners. The engines are also simpler in construction, much more efficient in the use of fuel, and a good deal more reliable in operation.

There is great concern today about noise and air pollution, and these new jet engines are sterling performers in both respects. At full power take-off, they leave barely a trace of smoke in their wake. As for noise, their full-throated roar has been hushed by more than 50 percent over the older engines. People living in communities near commercial airfields will certainly welcome this reduced strain on their eardrums.

The vastly improved jet engines on the Tristar are built by Rolls-Royce of England. This company has long designed and built some of the world's foremost automobile and aircraft engines.

Safety and comfort in airline travel today depend to a very large degree on the most modern flying instruments available. The Tristar has scores of the most advanced all-weather flight instruments now in existence. With the help of these instruments, pilots can bring this huge plane safely to earth even when bad weather causes near-zero visibility.

To relieve the pilot of some of the routine tasks of flying the Tristar jetliner on intercity air routes, the wide-bodied aircraft has an automatic navigation system. This is hooked up to the plane's automatic pilot so that the airplane's course and altitude are controlled without the need of human guidance.

Passenger comforts aboard the Tristar airliner have been given special attention by the plane's designers. The tunnel or tubelike effect of the interior, so common on the older planes, has been done away with on the Tristar. Its passenger cabin is squarish and more roomlike. Skillful use of indirect lighting and color have increased the feeling of spaciousness aboard the plane. Seats are wider and more comfortable. Wall cabinets on both sides of the cabin permit the storage of up to 40 pounds of carry-on luggage by each passenger.

Two wide aisles run the full length of the cabin. Three aisles extend across the cabin from one side to the other. These

This is the roomy interior of the L-1011.   *Lockheed-California Company*

shorter aisles connect to wide doorways on either side. The entryways and cross aisles make it easy for large numbers of passengers to get on or off the plane in a very short time. This is especially important in times of emergency when everyone must leave the aircraft as quickly as possible.

A truly unique feature of the Tristar jetliner is its lower deck area. This contains a galley for the storage and preparation of passenger meals and three insulated and heated compartments for baggage and cargo. The galley is 20 feet long and 6 feet high and is equipped with five high-speed infrared ovens, as well as refrigerators, freezers, storage cabinets, and food and beverage service carts. The infrared ovens are the newest in fast cooking equipment. They can cook steaks frozen at minus 10 degrees in 15 minutes. As a group, the ovens can prepare 270 meals in 30 minutes.

Two flight attendants work in the galley and they can get food and drink ready for up to 345 passengers in a very short time. The prepared passenger meals are sent to the main cabin above by means of two electrically operated lifts. The lifts are large enough to accommodate a food cart and cabin attendant.

Some airlines do not require all the cargo space available on the Tristar jetliner. They have therefore converted the forward section into a passenger lounge. For those air travelers who like to stretch their legs, the below-deck lounge can be reached by means of a short staircase.

Designed and built by Lockheed, the Tristar was first test flown on November 16, 1970. The Federal Aviation Administration, the U.S. government agency that checks all new aircraft for commercial service, gave its approval of the advanced jetliner on April 14, 1972. By the end of that month, on April 30, the huge jetliner was placed in regular service.

The design of the Tristar jetliner allows for changes to

meet different air travel needs in the future. Already newer models of the giant jet airliner are being planned. One of these is known as the L-1011-3. It will be a larger plane, capable of carrying 75 more passengers and of flying 1,000 miles farther. This newer Tristar is being considered mainly for use on long-distance intercontinental air routes.

PHYSICAL CHARACTERISTICS
Wingspan: 155 feet 4 inches.
Length: 178 feet 8 inches.
Height: 55 feet 4 inches (from tip of vertical tail to ground).
Fuselage width: 19 feet.
Weight without cargo: 238,817 pounds.
Cargo capacity: 45,750 pounds.
Passenger capacity: 250 to 400.
Speed: More than 600 miles per hour.
Cruising altitude: 33,000 feet.
Maximum range: 5,175 miles.
Engines: Three Rolls-Royce turbofan jet engines with a thrust of 45,000 to 50,000 pounds each.
Crew: The L-1011 is operated by a crew of three.

Directions for Making
the L-1011 Tristar Jetliner

Fuselage:
Trace and cut the fuselage as shown in the drawing (Plate 21). Notice that the vertical tail is included. These two parts of the giant jetliner are cut from a single piece of paper. Draw the design on both sides of the fuselage and tail. Try to do

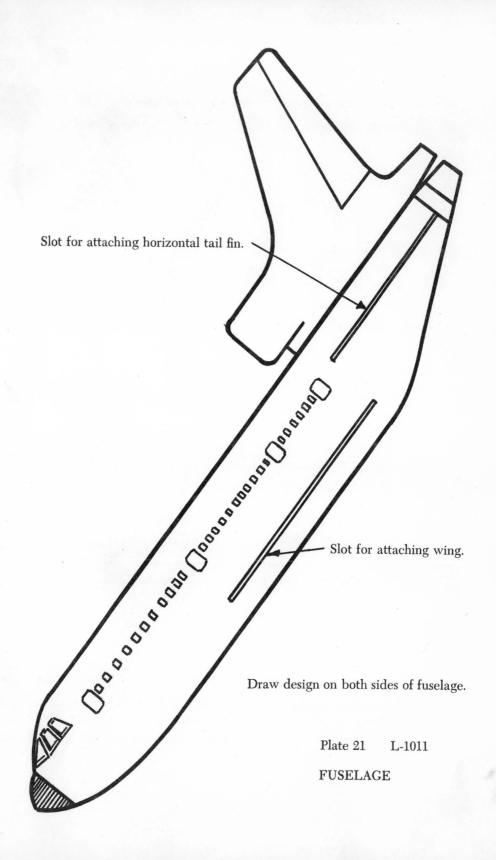

Slot for attaching horizontal tail fin.

Slot for attaching wing.

Draw design on both sides of fuselage.

Plate 21   L-1011

FUSELAGE

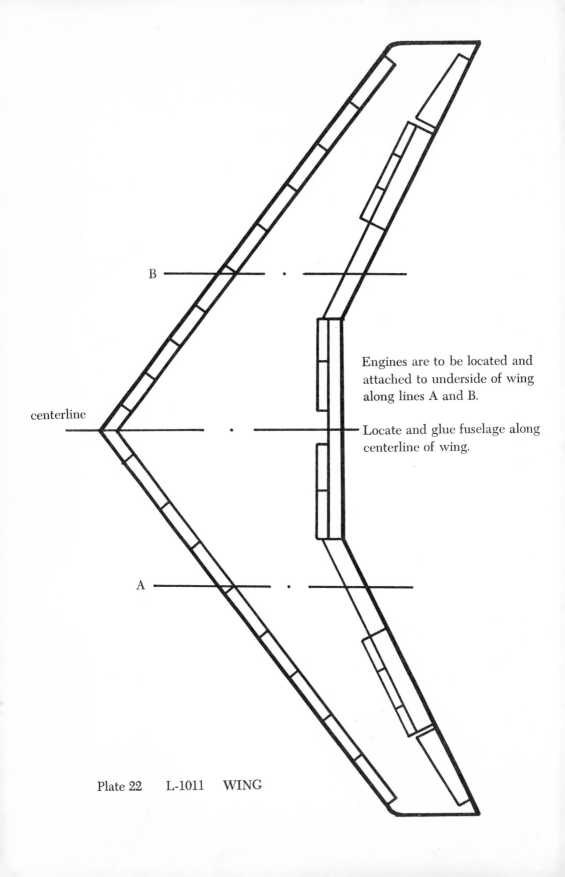

B

centerline

Engines are to be located and
attached to underside of wing
along lines A and B.

Locate and glue fuselage along
centerline of wing.

A

Plate 22   L-1011   WING

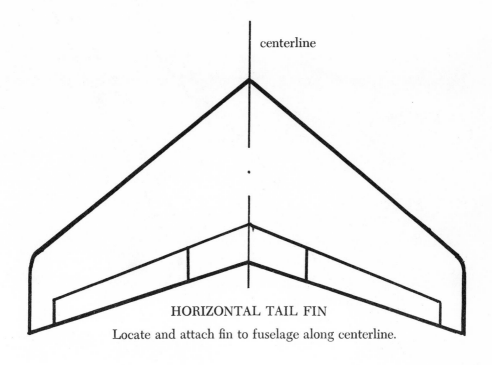

centerline

HORIZONTAL TAIL FIN
Locate and attach fin to fuselage along centerline.

Section of mount between points A and B is to be glued to underside of wing. Point A is to be at front edge of wing.

A   B

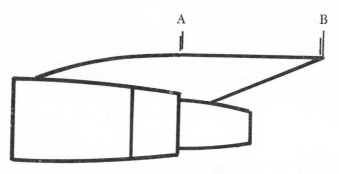

ENGINE AND MOUNT
Make two.

Plate 23   L-1011

this as carefully as you can since it will add to the attractive appearance of your finished model. Cut the two slots in the fuselage. The longer is for the wing and the shorter for the horizontal tail fin.

Wing:
Trace and cut the wing as shown in the drawing. (Plate 22). Be as careful as you can when doing this because it will help your model to fly better. Draw the design on the upper side of the wing only. Do not overlook the centerline. This is needed for accurately attaching the wing to the body.

Horizontal Tail Fin:
Trace and cut the horizontal tail fin, following the pattern (Plate 23). Draw the design on the upper and lower sides of the fin. Also draw the centerline on the fin. This will be helpful when you put your paper model together.

Engines and Mounts:
Use paper that is a little lighter in weight than that used for the fuselage and wing. Trace and cut two engines and mounts as shown in the drawing (Plate 23). Draw the design on both sides of the engines.

ASSEMBLING THE L-1011 TRISTAR
Attach the wing to the fuselage by sliding it through the longer slot. Put several spots of glue along the centerline. Hold the fuselage and the wing together for a few minutes until the glue hardens. Be careful when doing this, so that the fuselage and wing will be exactly at right angles to one another. If the body leans to one side or the other, this will not only detract from the good looks of your model but will interfere with its flying ability.

Next, glue the horizontal tail fin to the fuselage. Do this the same way that you attached the wing. Put several globs of glue along the centerline, slide the fin through the slot until the edge of the fuselage is exactly on the centerline, and hold for a few minutes until the glue hardens.

Finally, attach the two engines to the underside of the wing. See the pattern of the wing (Plate 22) for the proper location of the engines. Put glue along the top edges of the mounts and press these to the underside of the wing. Again, make certain that each of the engines is at a right angle to the wing. The appearance of your finished model will be spoiled if the engines are crooked.

Your Tristar paper model is now complete. If you did the job with care, you should have a model plane that flies with the greatest of ease and grace.

Model of the L-1011 Tristar jetliner.

The Russian Supersonic Transport TU-144

Supersonic military airplanes have been flying for many years. Now the first commercial air transports that can fly equally fast are coming into service. The Russian TU-144 was the first of this new breed of lightning-swift commercial planes to fly. It soared aloft on its maiden flight on December 31, 1968 and made the first-faster-than-the-speed-of-sound flight by a commercial transport on June 5, 1969.

Every line of the TU-144 emphasizes speed—the main reason for its creation. This is easily seen in the plane's needle-sharp nose, sharply swept-back wings, and gracefully curved vertical fin. The man chiefly responsible for bringing the TU-144 into existence was Dr. Alexei A. Tupolev, one of Russia's foremost designers of airplanes.

The wings of the TU-144 are the one feature that makes this supersonic transport different from most commercial aircraft. They are roughly triangular in shape when looked at from above. The forward portions of the wings start slightly behind the flight crew's compartment, then sweep back sharply

The Russian supersonic transport TU-144 looks like some prehistoric bird as it comes in for a landing. Notice how the nose is tilted downward so the pilot can see the runway.

in long curves toward the rear. The TU-144's wings were not shaped this way for artistic reasons. Mathematical calculations and wind tunnel tests on many different wing forms proved them to be the best shape for allowing the plane to fly both at supersonic speeds and also at very low speeds for landings.

When high-speed aircraft travel through the sky, air builds up along the front edge of the wings, creating friction and slowing the speed of the plane. This does not happen as quickly with the wings of the TU-144 because they are swept backward so sharply. It takes much longer for the air flow to build up and block the plane's forward speed. Hence, the plane can reach a speed of more than 1,500 miles per hour before the air flow begins to be a problem.

As we said, the wings of the TU-144 have also been designed for efficient flight at low speeds, as when the aircraft is coming in for a landing. In this maneuver, the plane comes down at a rather sharp angle, with its nose up and tail down. As the plane descends, an air bubble or cushion forms under the wings. The closer the TU-144 comes to earth, the stronger the force of the air cushion against the undersides of the wings. Thus, the giant plane has a kind of support for making a slow, gentle touchdown on the runway.

Another unusual feature of the TU-144 is its sharply pointed nose, which helps the plane knife through the air at supersonic speeds. But this is not so different from the front ends of supersonic military aircraft. They all have this kind of nose design. The different thing about the nose on the TU-144 is the fact that it is hinged and movable. The nose is dropped down for landings and take-offs and straightened out for speeding along in level flight.

The nose of the TU-144 has been made this way because of the sharp, nose-up angle at which the plane lands. The pilot would have great difficulty seeing the runway before him if the nose were fixed in a straight position. So during the landing procedure, the nose section drops downward, giving a clear view of the field ahead. After take-off when the plane is flying smoothly and swiftly in a normal manner, the pilot operates a control that lifts up and locks the nose section in place to give the body of the supersonic transport a smooth, unbroken appearance.

Unlike most planes, the TU-144 has no horizontal tail section with elevators for up and down maneuvers. Instead, it has elevons built into the rear edge of its sharply swept-back wings. These do the work of elevators and also help the pilot bank the plane when turning to the right or left.

Four very powerful jet engines drive the TU-144 at speeds in excess of 1,500 miles per hour. These huge power units have been clustered within a pod under the aircraft's body. The engines were placed in this position not only to help the plane fly efficiently, but also to make it easy for mechanics to reach them for servicing.

The interior of the TU-144 has been arranged to carry both first class and tourist class passengers. The forward part of the cabin is reserved for first class use and the remainder of the cabin for tourist. However, the sections are flexible so that, depending on passenger needs, they can be made larger or smaller. Between the first class and tourist sections is a galley where the flight attendants prepare food and drink for the passengers.

The passenger compartments of the TU-144 are sound-proof so that travelers hear little of the rumbling roar of the monster jet engines beneath the body of the plane. The passenger cabin has also been comfortably air-conditioned and pressurized to match earthbound atmospheric conditions as closely as possible. Since the swift transport normally travels at an altitude of more than twelve miles, this is of some importance for the safety and comfort of the passengers.

Capable of flying at a height of over 60,000 feet and at speeds slightly in excess of 1,500 miles per hour, the TU-144 as a commercial transport has truly impressive advantages. For example, a passenger who left the Moscow airport at noon of one day would arrive at nine o'clock in the morning of the same day at the airport in Montreal, Canada. The passenger would have been in the air for only five hours. Of course, it must be remembered in this time schedule that hours are gained going westward and lost traveling eastward. Nevertheless, the arrow-swift TU-144 makes close neighbors of the most distant cities on earth.

Because of its enormous speed, the TU-144 is said to be capable of doing the work of three ordinary jet airliners. This, of course, is true only for those air routes spanning several thousand miles. The supersonic transport is a great consumer of distance, and it performs to best advantage on routes that leap whole continents and oceans.

PHYSICAL CHARACTERISTICS

Wingspan: 90.7 feet.

Length: 191 feet.

Height: 37 feet (from tip of vertical tail fin to ground).

Weight without cargo: 395,000 pounds.

Cargo capacity: 26,400 pounds.

Passenger capacity: 120.

Top speed: 1,560 miles per hour.

Cruising altitude: 65,000 feet.

Maximum range: 4,560 miles.

Engines: Four jet engines. Each of the engines on the early models of the TU-144 had a power output of 38,580 pounds of thrust.

Crew: The TU-144 is operated by a flight crew of three.

Directions for Making the Russian SST TU-144

Fuselage:

Trace and cut the fuselage, following the pattern (Plate 24). Notice that this includes the vertical tail fin. These two parts of the plane are all one piece. Using black ink or crayon, or any color you wish, draw the design on both sides of the fuselage. Do this carefully because it will add to the realistic appearance of your completed model.

Wing:

Trace and cut the wing from the pattern (Plate 25) very carefully. This is important for making your model a good flyer. Do not omit the centerline, which will be needed when you

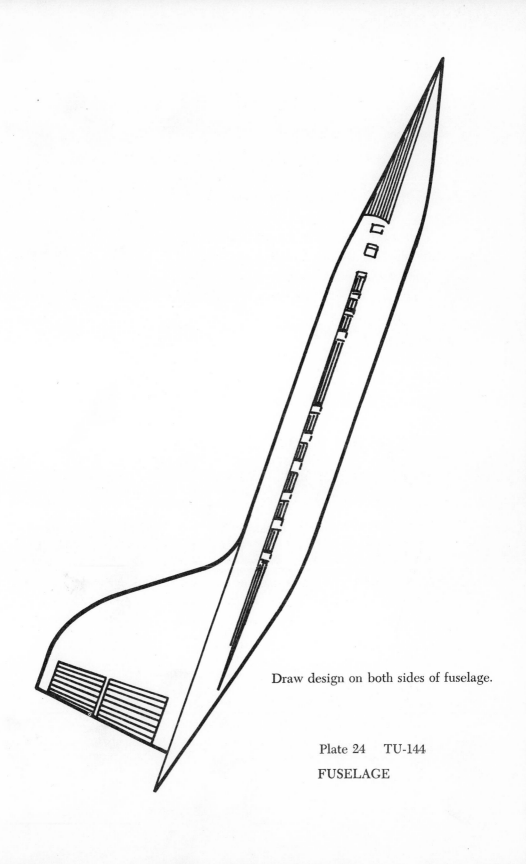

Draw design on both sides of fuselage.

Plate 24   TU-144

FUSELAGE

Plate 25   TU-144

WING

Locate and attach fuselage to wing along centerline.

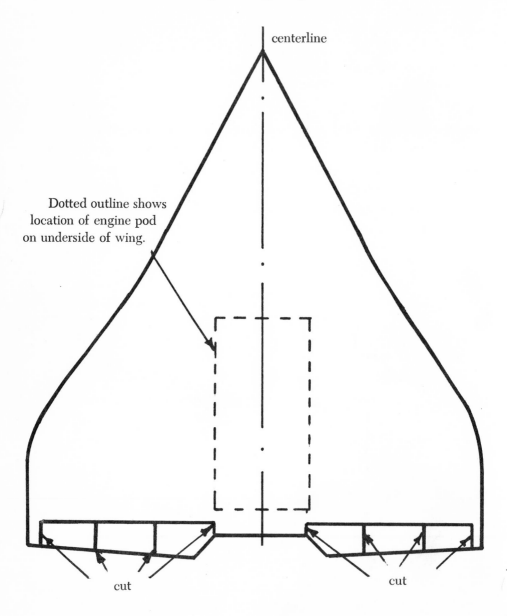

centerline

Dotted outline shows
location of engine pod
on underside of wing.

cut   cut

assemble the model. Draw the design on the rear edge of the wing just as it appears in the pattern. This represents the elevons which are needed for up and down maneuvers. Make small cuts on the sides of the elevons as indicated in the pattern. These will allow you to bend the elevons up or down so that your model can perform more maneuvers.

Engine Pod:

Make the engine pod from a single piece of paper that is lighter in weight than the paper you used for the fuselage and wing. Trace and cut the pattern as shown in the drawing (Plate 26). Fold along all the dotted lines. After you have made all the necessary folds, the pod should look like the end view in the drawing.

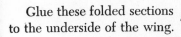

End view of engine pod will look like this when it is folded.

Glue these folded sections to the underside of the wing.

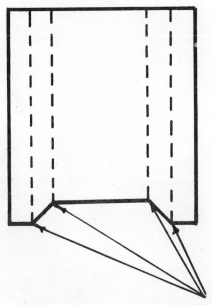

Plate 26   TU-144

ENGINE POD

Fold along dotted lines.

ASSEMBLING THE TU-144

Start assembling the TU-144 by joining the fuselage and wing. Put small amounts of glue along the centerline of the wing. Press the bottom edge of the fuselage onto the glued areas. Before gluing, be sure that you have the fuselage in the correct position; check the photo of the model for this. Also make sure the body is exactly at a right angle to the wing, and that it does not tilt to the right or left.

Next attach the engine pod to the underside of the body and wing. Put glue along the two longest edges of the pod and press it into place. Hold it onto the underside of the wing for a few moments until the glue hardens. This will complete your paper model.

Model of the TU-144 supersonic transport.

The Concorde
Supersonic Transport

A new and dramatic era in commercial air transport is dawning with the use of supersonic jetliners on the world's air routes. The Concorde is the second of these sleek, swift jetliners to be built and flown. The first was the Russian TU-144.

The Concorde is a product of the combined knowledge and skills of French and British aircraft manufacturers. The great cost of designing and building these very special airplanes makes it almost a necessity for aircraft builders to pool their resources and facilities.

The governments of France and England are also taking part in the project of building the Concorde. Their role is mainly to provide the needed money to support construction activities. France and England signed an agreement to support the Concorde project jointly on November 29, 1962. As a symbol of this international cooperative effort, it was decided to name the aircraft Concorde, meaning "agreement" or "harmony."

Long before France and England formally agreed to build

The Concorde SST is gracefully poised at the end of the runway for a take-off.   *Aerospatiale*

the Concorde, research leading to such an advanced aircraft had already been underway. In 1956 aeronautical scientists and engineers in both countries were hard at work with studies and tests on the best wing shape for a supersonic jetliner. They sought a design that was best suited for flying at speeds of better than 1,000 miles per hour as well as at slower speeds for landings. It was not an easy matter to combine these two features in one wing.

After several years of mathematical calculations, countless hours over the drawing boards, and innumerable wind tunnel tests, these aircraft design experts decided that a wing shaped very much like a triangle would be the most efficient. Their technical name for it was an ogee-planform delta wing. It was similar in shape to the wing which Russian designers had created for their TU-144 supersonic jetliner.

Concorde research studies also focused on the kind of metal needed for the plane's construction. Aircraft traveling at speeds of more than 1,000 miles per hour experience strains far greater than planes flying at less than half those velocities. Supersonic aircraft are also subject to high friction heat. This is caused by the tremendous speed of the air flowing over the aircraft. This can weaken ordinary aircraft metals and cause them to crack and break. So for much of the Concorde's structure new and stronger metal alloys were developed. These metals had to withstand safely both heat and stresses at high speeds.

Not the least important part of the early Concorde research had to do with the question of whether or not a supersonic jetliner had commercial value. It was concluded by those carrying out the study that the plane would definitely have a place in the international air transport business. They noted that business had increased in other transport systems—railroads, for example, and steamship lines—that had introduced newer and faster types of vehicles. The researchers felt confident that the same thing would happen when the supersonic jetliners were introduced into regular airline service.

Once all the basic design work for the Concorde was completed, actual construction of the aircraft began in 1964 in both French and English aircraft factories. The French model was designated the 001 and was the first Concorde to be completed. It was rolled out of the factory at Toulouse, France, on December 11, 1967. The plane's first test flight was made on March 2, 1969.

The unusual length of time between the completion of this first Concorde and its maiden flight was needed for thorough testing of the plane's complex structure and equipment. The builders of the supersonic airliner wanted to make as certain as possible that the plane's first flight would be a success.

Meanwhile the second Concorde to be finished, known as the 002, was finished and put through its test flight paces at Filton, England, on April 9, 1969.

Following an exhaustive series of preliminary test flights in which the Concorde proved itself a sound aircraft, preparations were begun to fly it at supersonic speed for the first time. This would be over 700 miles per hour. The Concorde successfully passed this test on October 1, 1969. Convinced now that their aircraft was a sterling sky performer, French pilots and engineers decided to send the Concorde winging to the top speed it was designed for, close to 1,400 miles per hour.

The day was November 4, 1970. The graceful aircraft stood for a few moments at the end of the runway. Then at the word from the control tower, the pilot opened the throttles wide. The powerful jet engines thundered as the Concorde began to roll forward. Halfway down the runway the sharp-nosed Concorde tilted upward at a steep angle and climbed swiftly toward the sky.

The pilot and copilot seated at the controls were calm but keenly alert, watching the countless instruments. Back in the cabin the technical observers were more tense as they kept their eyes glued to a speed indicator on the forward wall. This instrument showed the Concorde's swiftness in Mach numbers. Mach is the technical word for indicating the supersonic speed of aircraft. Mach 1 is the speed of sound—more than 700 miles per hour; Mach 2 is a supersonic rate of twice this speed.

The Concorde was flying swiftly against a deep blue sky more than ten miles above the earth. Steadily the pilot increased the engines' power. The needle on the Mach meter reached and passed the figure 1. There was only a slight shudder as the plane went through the sound barrier. The needle kept moving closer to the figure 2 as silence fell over the people in the cabin. All kept their eyes on the speed indicator. The Mach meter flashed a 2 and then slightly more, and a kind of hushed cheer rose from the passengers in the cabin. They were moving through the air at a speed of over 1,400 miles per hour with barely a physical sign of this tremendous velocity. There was no question now that the Concorde could do what its creators had expected of it.

The completion of the long series of subsonic and supersonic test flights did not mean that the Concorde was ready for regular commercial flights. Much more testing was planned to make sure that this new aircraft would transport passengers safely and swiftly to all corners of the earth. Accordingly, a long series of worldwide test flights was outlined for the Concorde. The tests were done for a number of reasons, not the least of which was the builders' desire to demonstrate to commercial airline operators what their speedy plane could do in the way of drastically shortening air distances.

Airports in Greece, Japan, the Philippines, and Australia, among others, all had visits from this swift sky courier. The United States had its glimpse of the Concorde in September of 1973 when the supersonic jetliner took part in ceremonies opening the mammoth new Dallas-Fort Worth Airport in Texas. On all its aerial journeys throughout the world, the Concorde slashed the normal air travel time by nearly half.

One other important reason for the Concorde's worldwide flights was to show aviation and nonaviation people alike that the plane's supersonic boom was not the fearsome thing they expected. When an aircraft flies through the sound barrier, reaching a speed of more than 700 miles per hour, shock waves are produced which sound like thunderclaps when they reach the ground. In addition to the sound, these waves have been known to crack walls in homes and break windows. Many people feel that supersonic commercial jetliners will be extremely damaging in this respect and do not wish to see them put into service.

However, the Concorde's world air travels left no trail of destruction. It entered and left airports much as conventional planes do, and with no more noise or air pollution. At those times when it was flown supersonically, the Concorde traveled over areas of the earth empty of inhabitants, thus making its supersonic boom harmless. This is what is planned for the plane's routes when it goes into commercial service.

The Concorde is sent zooming through the sky by four

powerful turbojet engines. These are mounted in pairs near the outer ends of the wings. The engines are built by Rolls-Royce of England and each of them produces more than 38,000 pounds of thrust. The full power of these engines, which can cause the ground to quiver in the vicinity of the Concorde, is used only for take-offs and when the plane is flying over ten miles above the earth at full speed.

The needle-sharp nose of the Concorde is similar to that of the Russian TU-144. Because of the odd way both of these supersonic planes have to land and take off—nose up, tail down—the front section is movable. It drops down for landings and take-offs so the pilot can see the runway. When the plane is in level flight, the nose is raised, converting the Concorde's entire body into a smooth, streamlined shape.

Although on the outside the Concorde looks radically different from conventional commercial jet planes, its cabin interior is much like the ordinary commercial jetliner. A center aisle separates twin seats on either side. These 144 seats can be so arranged that some are used for first class passengers and others for tourist travelers.

It is the hope of the Concorde's builders that the first supersonic jet will go into regular commercial service in 1975. The airlines expected to pioneer the use of these lightning-swift aircraft are British Overseas Airways Corporation and Air France. The planes are likely to be first flown on the North Atlantic air routes between Europe and America.

PHYSICAL CHARACTERISTICS
Wingspan: 83 feet 10 inches.
Length: 203 feet 9 inches.
Height: 37 feet 1 inch (from top of vertical tail to ground).
Weight without cargo: 389,000 pounds.
Cargo capacity: 28,000 pounds.
Passenger capacity: 144.

Top speed: 1360 to 1410 miles per hour, or Mach 2.05 to Mach 2.2.

Cruising altitude: 50,000 to 60,000 feet.

Maximum range: 4,000 miles.

Engines: Four Rolls-Royce turbojet engines of over 38,000 pounds of thrust each.

Crew: The Concorde is operated by a flight crew of three.

SUPERSONIC TIMETABLE

	Concorde hrs.-mins.	Subsonic hrs.-mins.	Time Saved hrs.-mins.
London-New York	3:30	7:05	3:35
Paris-Montreal	3:25	7:00	3:35
New York-Caracas	2:25	4:30	2:05
Los Angeles-Honolulu	2:30	5:15	2:45

Directions for Making the Concorde SST

Fuselage:

Trace and cut the fuselage very carefully, following the drawing (Plate 27). Remember to include the vertical tail section. This and the fuselage are made from a single piece of paper. Draw the design on both sides of the fuselage and vertical tail.

Wing:

Trace the wing as it is shown in the drawing (Plate 28) and cut it with extreme care. This will help your model to fly better and also make it look attractive. Draw the centerline on

Plate 27   Concorde

FUSELAGE

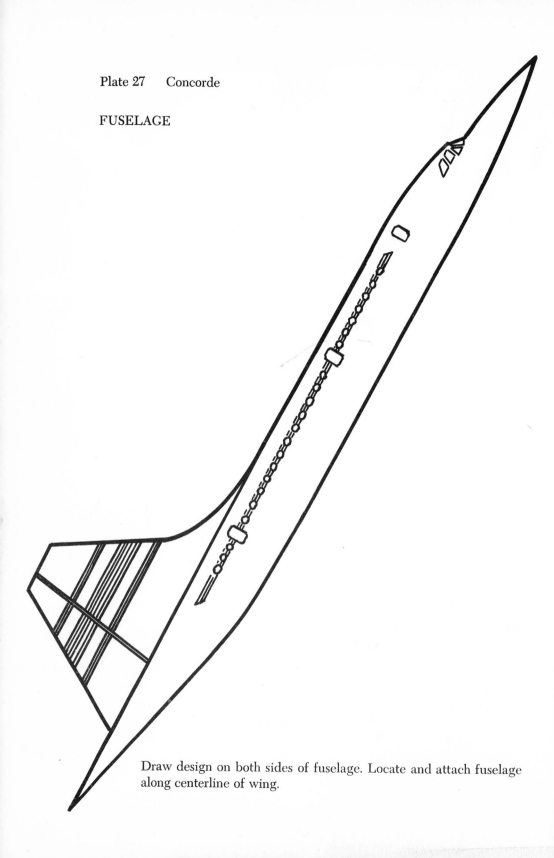

Draw design on both sides of fuselage. Locate and attach fuselage along centerline of wing.

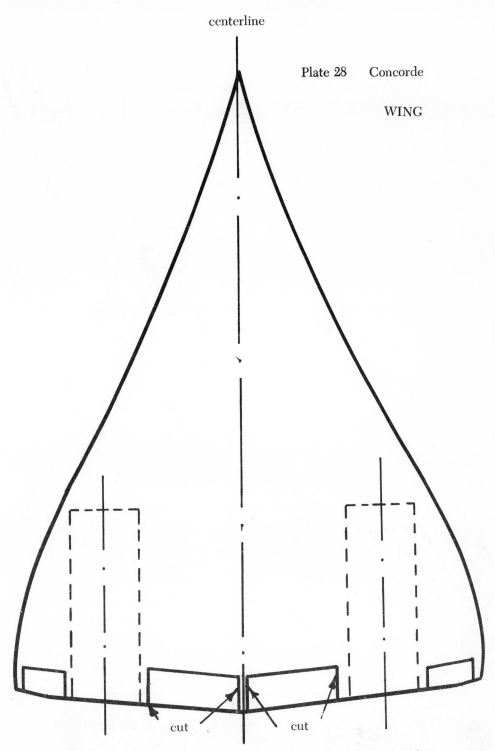

centerline

Plate 28   Concorde

WING

cut   cut

Dotted outlines show where engine pods are to be located and
glued to underside of wing.

the wing as shown. This is necessary for attaching the wing to the fuselage. Draw the design on the top side of the wing only. Draw engine pod locations on the wing.

Engine Pods:

Two engine pods are to be made for the Concorde model. Make these from paper that is lighter in weight than that used for the remainder of the model. Trace and cut them from the pattern (Plate 29). Fold the pods along the dotted lines to make a kind of boxlike structure. The engine pods are much like the one you made for the Russian TU-144 supersonic transport. Try to make the pods as neat as possible so they will add to the attractiveness of your finished model. These will complete the parts needed for your flying paper model Concorde.

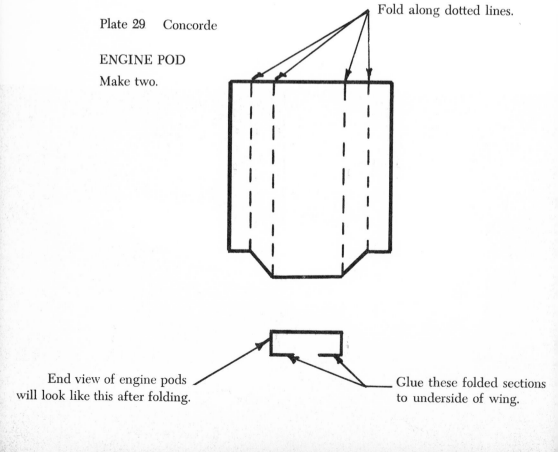

Plate 29   Concorde

ENGINE POD
Make two.

Fold along dotted lines.

End view of engine pods will look like this after folding.

Glue these folded sections to underside of wing.

ASSEMBLING THE CONCORDE

Start putting your Concorde model together by placing several spots of glue along the centerline of the wing. Allow the glue to set for a few moments until it is tacky. Next, press the bottom edge of the fuselage onto the glued spots on the wing. Be careful when doing this. Keep the fuselage exactly on the centerline. Also make sure that it does not lean to the right or left. Hold the fuselage in position for a few moments until the glue hardens.

The engine pods on the Concorde are attached next. Unlike the engine pod on the Russian SST, those on the Concorde are fixed to the underside of the wing out near the tips. See the wing pattern for the correct position of the pods. It will be easier for you to attach the engine pods if you turn the model upside down.

Your Concorde flying paper model is now complete. Be careful when you fly it. Do not create any sonic booms—you might crack the windows!

Model of the Concorde supersonic transport.

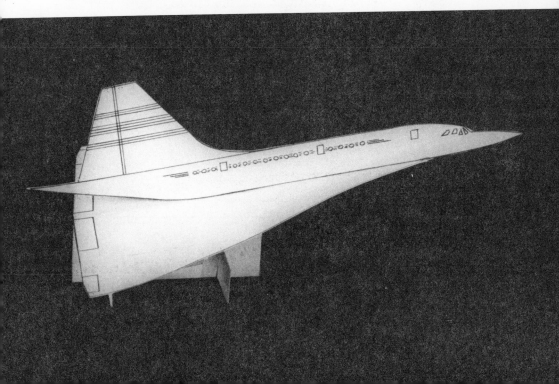

WINGS OF TOMORROW

Aeronautical scientists and engineers are constantly busy with new ideas for building faster airplanes or aircraft that fly in a new, more efficient manner. Designing aircraft for the future is slow, tedious work. From the earliest idea stage, through design, construction, and experimental flight, the development of a new airplane can easily take from ten to fifteen years.

The aircraft talked about in the pages ahead are for the most part only ideas. They are very much in the drawing board or design stage. Only one at the moment is in the experimental flying stage—the X-24B lifting body. This will soon be joined by another, the space shuttle. The rest are not expected to take to the skies until the twenty-first century. They will be real speedsters, flashing through the fringe of outer space at from 3,500 to more than 7,000 miles per hour. These are so-called hypersonic speeds, at which the airplane body heats up to an extremely high temperature.

The futuristic shapes of these advanced aircraft make wonderful paper airplane models. They are simple to make with excellent flying qualities.

The X-24B Lifting Body

The X-24B is strictly an experimental plane (hence the prefix X) that is helping aeronautical scientists and engineers to prove out their ideas for aircraft able to fly at hypersonic speeds.

Both the U.S. Air Force and the National Aeronautics and Space Administration are supporting the research work on the X-24B. For the Air Force, this experimental plane is expected to lead to the design and construction of super-swift military aircraft; for NASA, the X-24B may show the way to commercial air transports of tomorrow with ten times the speed of those now flying.

The X-24B is the second experimental model of its type. This is indicated by the letter B. The first model, X-24A, did not perform to the satisfaction of the aeronautical experts. So they went back to their drawing boards and wind tunnel test models for new design features. Of major concern was a new wing shape to help the plane fly better at both super speeds and the low speeds vital for landing.

The name "lifting body" given the X-24B comes from the

The wingless experimental plane X-24B is called a lifting body. Its body provides a lifting force just as a wing does on a conventional airplane.   *Martin Marietta Aerospace*

shape of its body. This has been designed to perform in much the same manner as the wings of conventional aircraft. Its shape is such that as the vehicle moves through the air, a lifting force acts on its under and upper surfaces to keep it airborne. Thus, the X-24B has its wings and body combined in one single structure.

In appearance, the X-24B resembles a giant arrowhead. Its nose is sharply pointed while the sides, that would ordinarily be the front edges of a conventional wing, sweep backward at an acute angle. To help control the X-24B's directional flight, three vertical fins are attached to its tail end.

For propelling the X-24B on its experimental flights, a single powerful rocket engine is installed in its tail section. The craft also has two rocket engines of less power which are used by the test pilot to help slow the vehicle's speed during landing maneuvers. The test program calls for a gradual increase in the aircraft's speed as its flying qualities become better understood. So far it has been flown at a speed of slightly more than 1,000 miles per hour.

During test flights the X-24B does not take off from the ground like an ordinary aircraft. Instead, it is hooked onto the underside of the wing of a huge B-52 bomber, taken to an altitude of 45,000 feet, and released. At the moment of separation from the mother plane, the test pilot on the X-24B switches on the main rocket engine, then zooms skyward to a height of 60,000 feet and a speed of about 1,000 miles per hour.

Because a rocket engine uses an enormous amount of fuel in a very short time, the test flight is brief. When the main rocket engine shuts off, the pilot guides his craft back to earth in a gliding maneuver. To slow his speed for better landing control, the pilot fires the aircraft's smaller rocket engines. They act in a reverse direction to that of the main rocket engine, pushing against the airplane to slow its forward speed.

The X-24B lands with its nose slanting upward at a sharp angle. This permits an air cushion to build up beneath its body which helps to slow the aircraft's descent. The experimental aircraft lands at a speed of 200 miles per hour and uses up about one mile of runway before rolling to a stop.

Because of the work carried out with the X-24B, a new breed of airplane—more accurately, flying vehicle—will one

During test flights the X-24B is carried by a giant B-52 bomber to a height of 40,000 feet and then released to fly on its own. The experimental aircraft is the first of many that will be able to fly in space and in the earth's atmosphere. *Martin Marietta Aerospace*

day be created. These aircraft of tomorrow will be capable of journeying through the earth's atmosphere as well as through the lower region of outer space.

PHYSICAL CHARACTERISTICS

Width: 19 feet 2 inches.

Length: 37 feet 6 inches.

Height: 10 feet 4 inches.

Weight: without fuel—7,800 pounds; with fuel—13,000 pounds.

Speed: Slightly over 1,000 miles per hour.

Altitude: 70,000 feet.

Range: In its present experimental stage, the lifting body stays close to its landing field.

Engines: One main rocket engine, XLR-11, with 8,000 pounds of thrust; two smaller rocket engines, each with 400 pounds of thrust.

Crew: One pilot operates the X-24B.

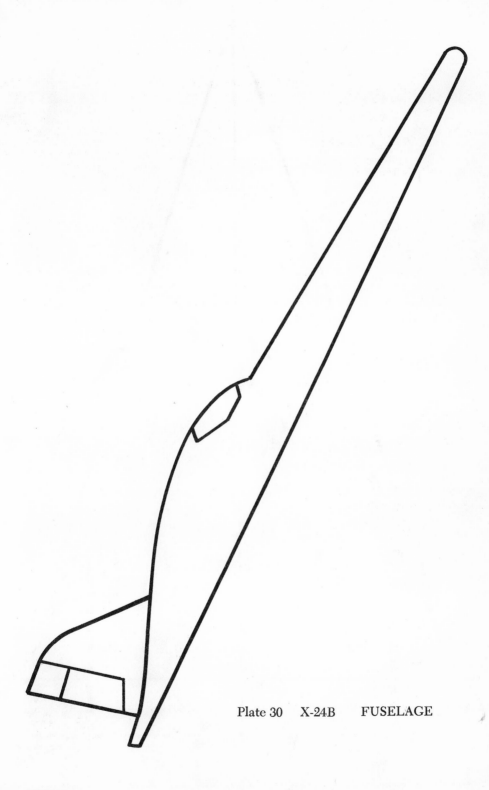

Plate 30   X-24B   FUSELAGE

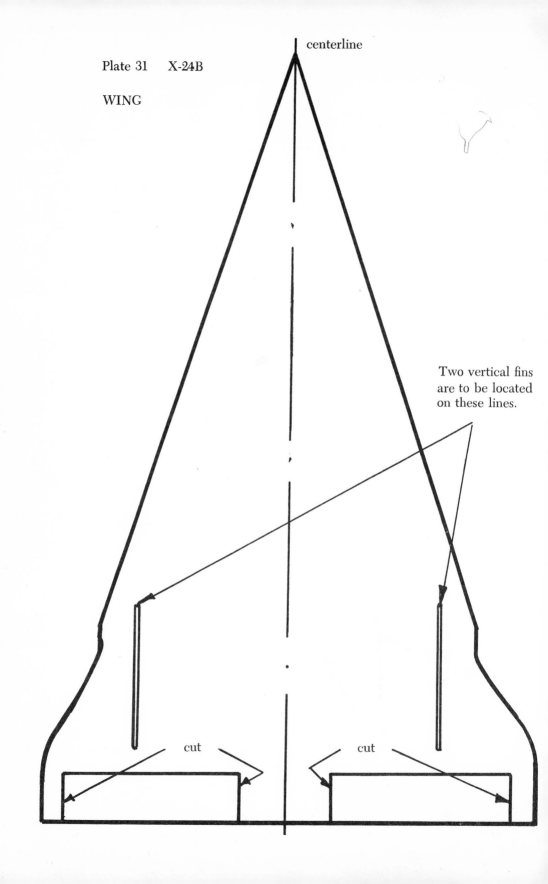

centerline

Plate 31   X-24B

WING

Two vertical fins
are to be located
on these lines.

cut

cut

Directions for Making
the X-24B Lifting Body

Fuselage:

Trace and cut the body as shown in the pattern (Plate 30). Be sure to include a single vertical fin. Using black ink, or black crayon, draw the cockpit canopy as it appears on the pattern.

Wing:

Trace and cut the wing as it appears in the drawing (Plate 31). Draw the centerline. This will be needed for gluing the body and wing together. Also draw the two short lines near the rear of the wing. The experimental airplane's two additional vertical fins are to be glued on these lines. Draw the outlines of the flaps at the rear edge and make cuts as indicated.

Vertical Fins:

Trace and cut two vertical fins, following the pattern (Plate 32). Include the design on both sides of the fins. Note the gluing tab along the bottom edge of the fin. The tabs are needed for attaching the fins to the plane.

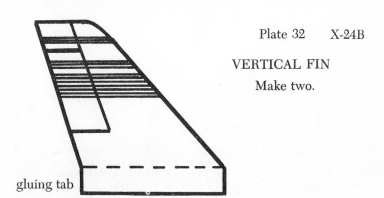

Plate 32   X-24B

VERTICAL FIN
Make two.

gluing tab

Bend on dotted line so tab will be on inside of fin when attached
to the wing. Bend fins slightly toward wing tips after they are firmly glued.

ASSEMBLING THE X-24B

Glue the fuselage to the wing. Use the centerline on the wing as a guide for getting the body in a straight line with respect to the wingtips. The body must be in an absolutely straight position. Hold the body in position for a few moments until the glue hardens.

Next, glue the two vertical fins onto the wing. Locate these on the two lines drawn near the rear portion of the wing. Bend the gluing tabs along the dotted lines so each tab is toward the center tail fin.

Notice that the fins should bend outward slightly as on the real aircraft. Check the photo of the real X-24B to see how the vertical fins should look. The X-24B will now be ready for its series of test flights.

Model of the X-24B lifting body.

The Mach 6
Hypersonic Commercial Jetliner

The hypersonic airliner is only a drawing board model of tomorrow's aircraft. Its design features are still temporary. Aeronautical scientists and engineers are continuing to replace ideas for the vehicle's performance with others they feel will improve its flying qualities. In brief, it is very much a twenty-first-century product at the moment.

Despite the constant changes being made, this particular hypersonic airliner is expected to have some truly mind-spinning features. The speed of this aircraft is in the Mach 6 range, or better than 4,000 miles per hour. It will fly at its maximum speed at the fringe of outer space—an altitude of about 110,000 feet. In size it will be comparable to one of the jumbo jets now in commercial service, with room for 300 passengers. The propulsion units of the hypersonic transport will enable it to span a distance of 5,000 nautical miles in minutes.

Perhaps the most different thing about this particular hypersonic airliner will be the fuel for its engines. Designers expect it to use liquid hydrogen, rather than the oil-based fuel cur-

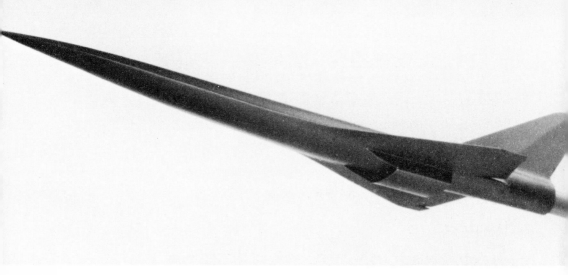

This is a wind tunnel model of a Mach 6 airliner of the twenty-first century. The proposed hypersonic air transport would cruise at a speed of more than 3,500 miles per hour and an altitude of over 100,000 feet. *NASA*

rently burned by commercial jetliners. Liquid hydrogen is not only a more effective fuel with respect to the amount of power to be derived from it, but it will be vitally important as petroleum shortages become continuously more critical. The supply of hydrogen is nearly limitless. The ocean waters, for example, are just one enormous source, covering almost 80 percent of the earth's surface.

Another feature of this hypersonic airliner that will make it different from those now in service is the metal to be used in its construction. This will be stronger than present-day aircraft metals in order to withstand the enormous stresses and strains of the plane's great speed. More importantly, the new metal alloys now being developed will retain their strength while heating up to extremely high temperatures.

The heat generated in the structure of a hypersonic airliner is an important problem that designers of tomorrow's aircraft have to consider and solve. The plane's friction heat will result from air molecules sliding over the body and wings. The metal must hold its strength under extremely high temperatures; otherwise it would bend and crack, and the aircraft would be destroyed. The same heat problem had to be overcome for the spacecraft in which the American astronauts rode back through the earth's atmosphere after journeying to the moon.

Directions for Making the Mach 6 Hypersonic Commercial Jetliner

Fuselage:
Trace and cut the fuselage as shown in the drawing (Plate 33). Draw the windows on both sides of the body.

Wing:
Trace and cut the wing, following the pattern (Plate 34). Include the centerline in your drawing. This will help you when you put the model together. Draw the flaps along the trailing edge of the wing. Cut the short sides of each flap so you can bend it up or down. Bending the flaps in this manner can help your model fly in climbing or downward gliding maneuvers.

Vertical Tail Fin:
Trace and cut the vertical tail fin as shown in the pattern (Plate 35). Be sure to include the gluing tabs. Draw the design on both sides of the fin.

ASSEMBLING THE MACH 6
Glue the vertical tail fin to the rear portion of the fuselage between points A and B, as indicated on the pattern. Glue one of the gluing tabs to each side of the fuselage. Then hold the tail fin in place for a few moments until the glue sets.

Next, attach the fuselage to the wing. Put a substantial

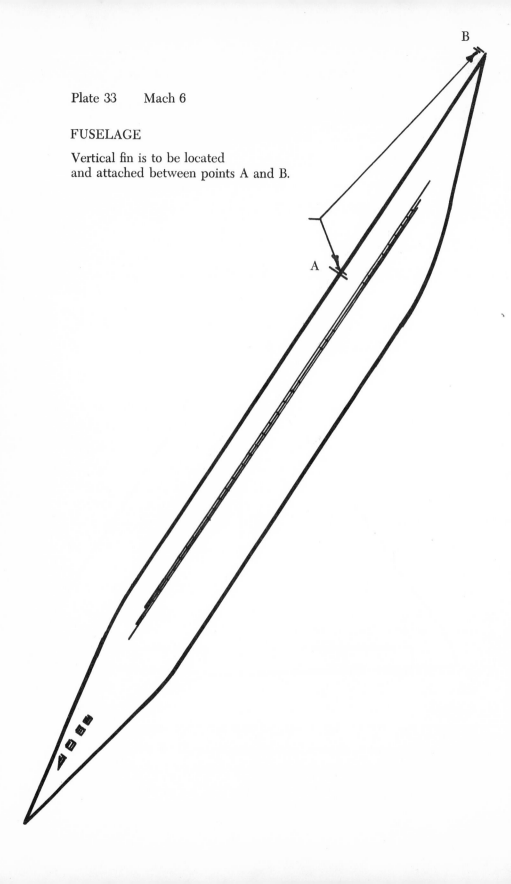

Plate 33   Mach 6

FUSELAGE

Vertical fin is to be located
and attached between points A and B.

Plate 34   Mach 6

WING

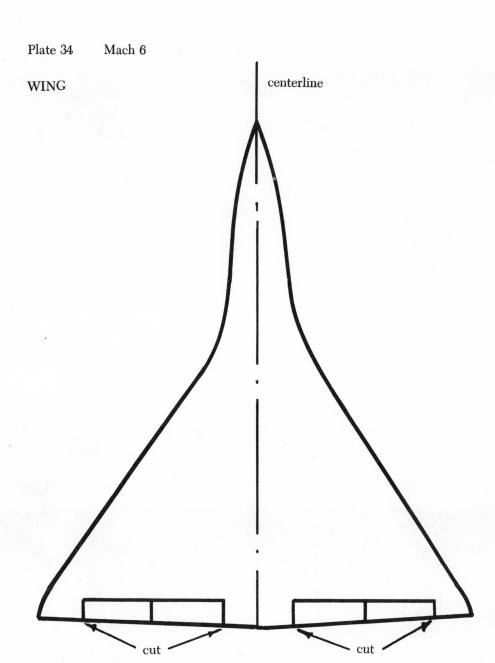

centerline

cut

cut

Join wing and body along centerline.

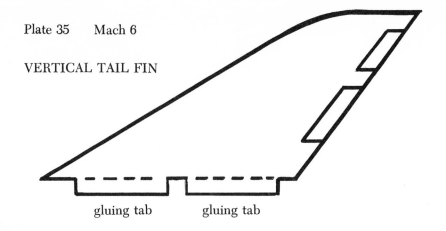

Plate 35   Mach 6

VERTICAL TAIL FIN

gluing tab   gluing tab

amount of glue along the bottom edge of the fuselage. Press the fuselage onto the wing along the centerline, making sure it is straight with respect to the tips of the wing. Also make certain that the body remains upright and does not lean to one side or the other.

This is all there is to putting your model of the hypersonic jetliner together. You are now ready to fly it and listen to that sonic boom!

Model of the Mach 6 hypersonic jetliner.

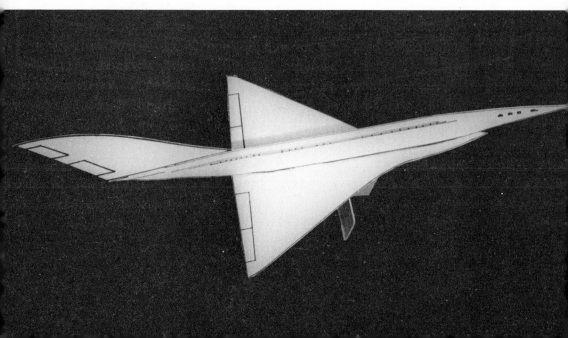

The Mach 10
Hypersonic Transport

The Mach 10 hypersonic transport is strictly an idea airplane. Its features are still being worked on by designers. There is much to do in the way of developing new and more powerful jet engines, creating stronger materials, and even deciding what the final aerodynamic shape of the vehicle will be. Whatever its ultimate characteristics, the hypersonic transport will be an air vehicle for the twenty-first century.

As aerodynamic scientists and engineers conceive this hypersonic air vehicle at the moment, its design could be adapted for a strategic bomber with a speed in the Mach 12 range; it could serve as a commercial transport with a speed range of from Mach 8 to Mach 10; or it could be developed for use as a launch vehicle with a speed of better than Mach 10. If created for this latter purpose, the hypersonic transport would carry a manned spacecraft to a height of over 100,000 feet, where the spacecraft would detach from the mother plane and continue on into space under its own power.

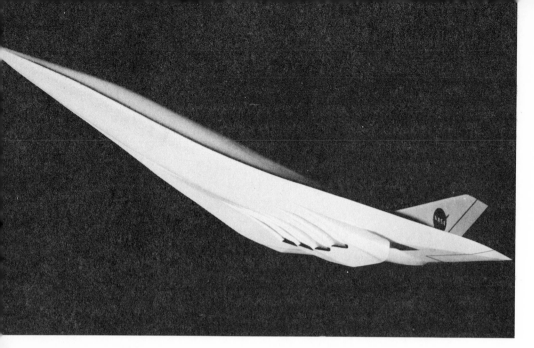

A hypersonic Mach 10 commercial airliner flying at a speed of 7,000 miles per hour may one day look like this wind tunnel model.

To propel the Mach 10 hypersonic air vehicle at speeds of more than 7,000 miles per hour, a combination battery of six turbojet engines and six ramjet engines would be employed. These power units would be housed in a single streamlined pod on the underside of the aircraft.

The six turbojet engines would be used by the plane for take-offs and acceleration almost to its top speed. These engines would also be employed for low landing speeds. The ramjet engines would be switched on to propel the aircraft to its maximum speed and altitude.

Only a few of the Mach 10 hypersonic transport's design features have been firmly established. Nevertheless, for the model maker it is a beautiful subject even at this early stage of development. Its streamlined shape is ideal for making a flying paper model. So let's not wait for the twenty-first century when the real aircraft will appear. Let's build our own right now!

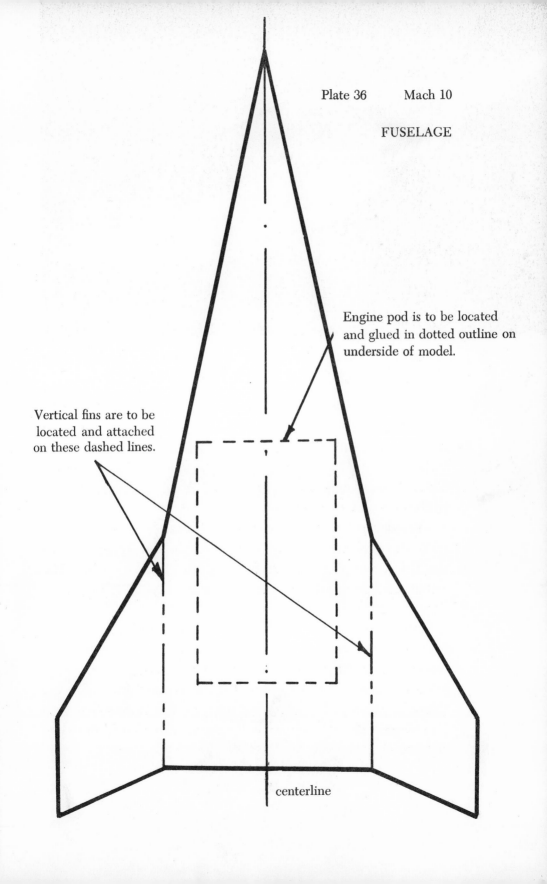

Plate 36   Mach 10

FUSELAGE

Engine pod is to be located
and glued in dotted outline on
underside of model.

Vertical fins are to be
located and attached
on these dashed lines.

centerline

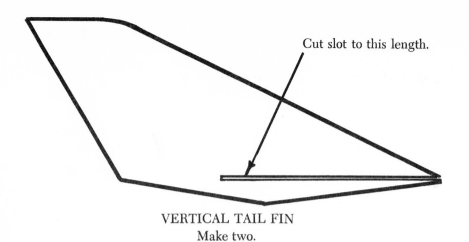

Cut slot to this length.

VERTICAL TAIL FIN
Make two.

Plate 37   Mach 10

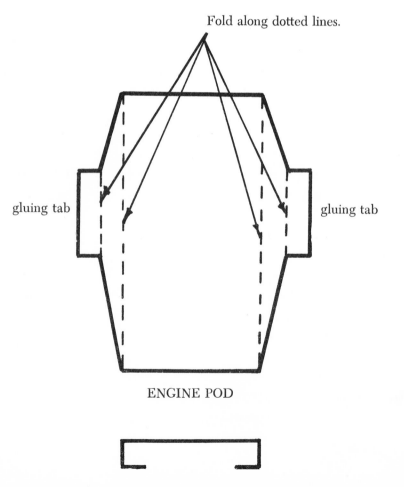

Fold along dotted lines.

gluing tab   gluing tab

ENGINE POD

End view of engine pod will look like this after folding

Directions for Making
the Mach 10
Hypersonic Transport

Fuselage:

The fuselage and wings of the Mach 10 hypersonic transport are one unit. The unit is shaped like an arrowhead. Trace and cut as shown in the pattern (Plate 36).

On the underside of the model, mark the place where the engine pod is to be located and glued. Also mark the locations for attaching the two vertical fins on the upper side.

Vertical Tail Fins:

Trace and cut two tail fins from the pattern (Plate 37). Cut a slot in each tail fin as indicated. These are for attaching the fins to the main section of the plane.

Engine Pod:

To make the pod, use paper that is lighter in weight than that used for the rest of the model. Trace and cut the engine pod as shown in the pattern. (Plate 37).

ASSEMBLING THE MACH 10

Putting together the Mach 10 hypersonic transport model is simple. Start by folding the engine pod along the dotted lines. Put glue on the gluing tabs of the pod and attach the pod to the underside of the model in the area you have marked.

Next, attach the two vertical tail fins. Put several dabs of glue along the lines on the fuselage where the fins are to be located. Slide the fins onto the body, using the slots. Make sure the fins are absolutely at right angles to the body. They should not lean to the right or left. By keeping the fins straight, you will make the appearance of your finished model considerably more attractive, and the model will also fly better.

The Mach 10 hypersonic transport is now complete and ready for launching. If you wish, you may draw your own designs on the finished model. The best places to add these are on the vertical fins.

Model of the Mach 10 hypersonic transport.

The Space Shuttle

The present method of sending manned and unmanned vehicles into space is enormously expensive. The main reason for this is the one-time use of the huge rockets that launch the spacecraft from earth. Once the rockets and space vehicles have done their jobs, they are gone forever.

The space shuttle is being developed to eliminate this costly technique. The shuttle will consist of a manned, reusable orbiting vehicle. It will be mounted piggyback fashion onto a large expendable propellant tank and a pair of solid propellant rockets that can be recovered and reused. After the two launch rockets have served their purpose, they will come back to earth undamaged, and the shuttle will continue on into space.

At the time of launching, the shuttle's three liquid rocket engines will be ignited along with the two solid launch rockets. When an altitude of about 25 miles has been reached, the two solid rocket engines will separate from the shuttle. They will parachute to the ocean below and be picked up by a recovery ship. Meanwhile the shuttle's own engines will take the vehicle and the attached propellant tank into low earth orbit.

This artist's drawing shows how the space shuttle will look orbiting the earth. Off to the left is a small working satellite.   *NASA*

Just before the desired orbit has been attained, the propellant tank will be detached from the shuttle. The tank's firing retrorockets will slow its speed and it will drop out of orbit into the sea below. The huge tank will not be recovered.

The space shuttle with its crew of three will be capable of staying in orbit for a normal 7-day period. If necessary, the time in space can be extended to 30 days. After the shuttle's mission is over, its crew will fire a series of small retrorockets that will slow the speed of the space vehicle. The shuttle will drop out of orbit and head for earth. The crew will guide the spacecraft to a landing just as though it were a conventional jetliner. After it has been serviced, the shuttle will be ready for a return trip into space.

The space shuttle is in an advanced state of design. The first test flights of the vehicle are expected to be made in 1976. Two years thereafter it is hoped the spacecraft will be ready for its first journey into space.

The space shuttle will be an impressive-looking vehicle. In size and weight it will compare to a modern jumbo jetliner, like the DC-10. The shuttle will weigh about 150,000 pounds without fuel. From nose to tail end it will measure 123 feet. Its triangular, delta-shaped wing will span 78 feet from tip to tip. The cargo area of the shuttle, directly in back of the crew's quarters, will extend 60 feet in length and some 15 feet in diameter.

Three main rocket engines will be installed in the tail end of the shuttle. Propellant for these engines will come from the external tank that will be dropped from the spacecraft once orbit is reached. The shuttle will also have a system of smaller rockets mounted in external pods above each of the wing tips. These rockets will allow the crew to change the orbit of the shuttle if necessary, will help get the vehicle into final orbit, and will permit the crew to maneuver the shuttle into position for docking with another orbiting spacecraft. The most important job to be performed by these smaller rockets, perhaps, will be to get the shuttle out of orbit and to prepare it for landing on earth.

The cabin of the space shuttle will have room for three regular flight crew members. There will also be space for four additional individuals who may be aboard as passengers headed for an assignment with an orbiting space station. The crew's area will be divided into three sections. The flight section will be the uppermost compartment of the cabin, containing almost all the controls for operating the spacecraft. Directly beneath the flight section will be room for such items as crew accommodations, flight equipment, waste management and food management apparatus, and the airlock. The latter will be used by crew members for transferring to an orbiting space station. The crew will eat, sleep, and exercise in a central area of the shuttle. Finally, the third section will carry the shuttle's main equipment, such as its three rocket engines.

The shuttle is expected to be useful for a variety of space assignments. It can serve as a connecting link between an orbiting space station and the earth, bringing supplies, equipment, and even a replacement crew. The shuttle may also be used for servicing an orbiting unmanned weather or communications satellite. In this case the shuttle could bring up another satellite in good working order to take the place of one that is not operating. The space shuttle will be able to perform rescue missions in space if any difficulties arise aboard an orbiting space station or other manned space vehicle.

The space shuttle promises to be a versatile, valuable performer in money-saving, practical space activities.

Directions for Making the Space Shuttle

Fuselage:

Trace and cut the body as shown on the drawing (Plate 38). Draw the black area on the nose. On the real space shuttle this is for reducing glare on the eyes of the crew. Draw the two thick lines near the tail section. These are needed for locating and attaching the vertical tail fin.

Wing:

Trace and cut the wing as it appears in the pattern (Plate 39). Draw the sections on the rear edge of the wing to make the flaps and make cuts as indicated.

It will be helpful for assembling the model to draw a centerline on the wing. This will permit you to position the body correctly.

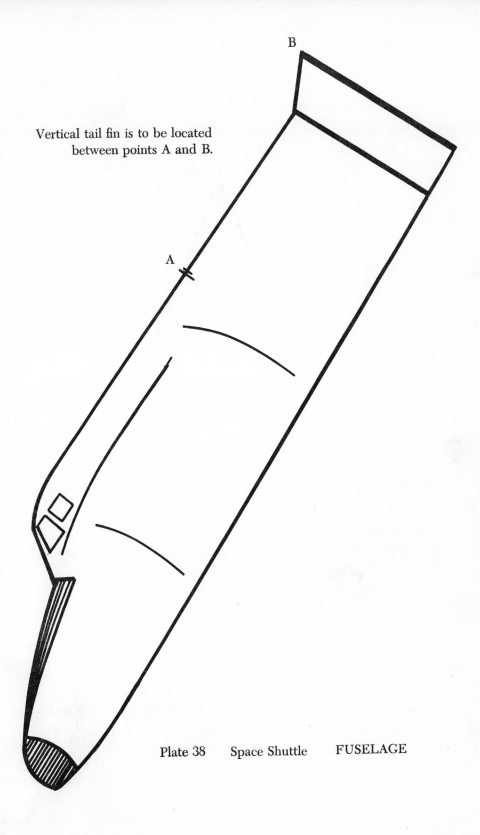

Vertical tail fin is to be located
between points A and B.

B

A

Plate 38   Space Shuttle   FUSELAGE

Plate 39   Space Shuttle

WING

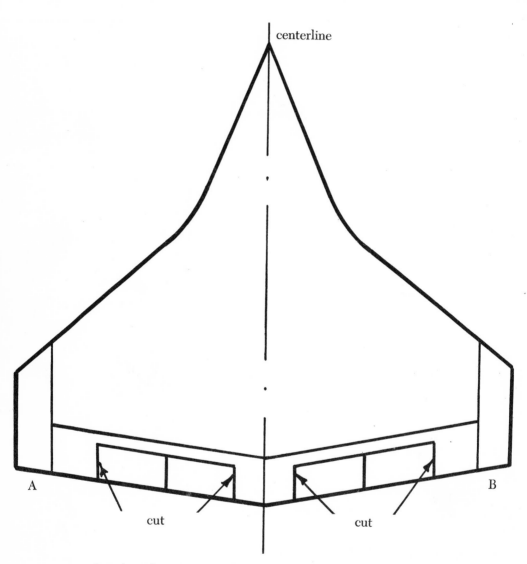

Attach rocket engine pods A and B to wing tips as indicated.

Plate 40   Space Shuttle

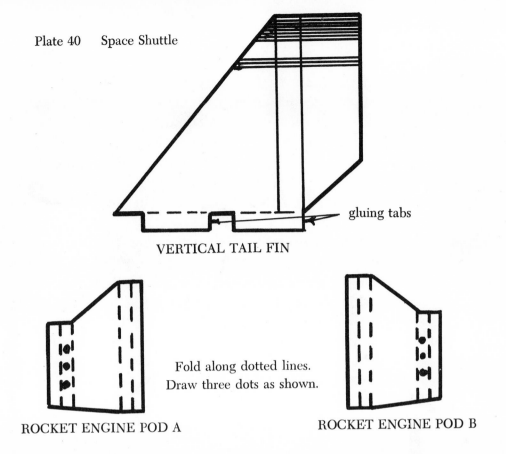

gluing tabs

VERTICAL TAIL FIN

ROCKET ENGINE POD A

Fold along dotted lines.
Draw three dots as shown.

ROCKET ENGINE POD B

End view of rocket engine pods
will look like this after folding.

Glue to wing.

Glue to wing.

Vertical Tail Fin:

Trace and cut the vertical tail fin as shown (Plate 40).
Draw the vertical lines which indicate the rudder. Also draw
the design at the top of the flap.

Rocket Engine Pods A and B:

Trace and cut the pattern for each of the pods. (Plate 40).
Fold along the dotted lines of the patterns. Draw three black
dots on each pattern as indicated. These represent the exhaust
vents of the rocket engines.

ASSEMBLING THE SPACE SHUTTLE

Start putting your model together by gluing the body to the wing. Place several spots of glue along the centerline of the wing. Place the lower edge of the body along the centerline and hold it upright for several minutes until the glue hardens. Do not allow the body to tilt to the right or left. If this happens, your model will not only fly poorly but will also look sloppy.

Next, glue the vertical tail fin in position. Locate this along the two thick lines which you drew on the body. Glue one gluing tab on each side of the body, and hold the fin in as upright a position as possible until the glue hardens.

Finally, glue the rocket engine pods A and B to the top surface of each wing tip. Pod A is glued on the left wing tip (when model is viewed from the tail end): pod B is glued to the right wing tip.

This will complete your model of the space shuttle. It is now ready for launching into orbit.

Model of the space shuttle.

Glossary

Ailerons: These are movable sections on the trailing or rear edge of an aircraft wing. They are operated by the pilot during turning maneuvers. Ailerons help keep the plane in perfect balance while turning to the right or left. When an aircraft banks during a turn, one wing tip is tilted lower than the other. If the plane is turned to the left, the left wing tip is lower than the right wing tip. The opposite occurs when the plane turns to the right. Ailerons are moved opposite to one another—that is, one is tilted up and the other down, depending on the desired turning maneuver.

Airfoil: This is the technical word used to describe the cross section of an airplane wing. The particular shape of the airfoil largely determines an airplane's flying characteristics, such as speed, altitude, range, and maneuverability.

Center of gravity: The center of gravity—CG for short—is a hypothetical but critical point in an aircraft. It is the point in an aircraft's structure at which, if the plane were supported at that point, it would be in perfect balance. If the weight of an airplane is too great on either side of the center of gravity, the aircraft will be a very poor flyer if, indeed, it does not end up a wreck. You can find the CG of your paper plane models by balancing them on your extended index finger.

Dihedral: When the wings of an aircraft angle upward from the horizontal when the aircraft is seen from the front, they are said to have a dihedral angle.

Elevators: Elevators are attached to the horizontal stabilizer. These are tail sections that move upward and downward. The elevators permit the pilot to maneuver the plane in an upward climb or downward dive. Elevators are moved in unison, up or down.

Elevons: Elevons are movable panels on the rear edge of a wing. They do the combined work of conventional ailerons and elevators. Elevons are generally used on airplanes having delta-shaped wings, like those of supersonic transports.

Fuselage: This is the technical word for the body of an airplane.

Horizontal stabilizer: This is one of the major parts of an airplane's tail structure. It is also commonly referred to as the horizontal fin (as in this book). The horizontal stabilizer helps to keep the plane flying in an even or horizontal position.

Hypersonic: This is a speed range far higher than supersonic. The body and wing of an air or space vehicle traveling at hypersonic speed heat up to a high temperature.

Lift: Lift is the force acting on an airplane's wings and body that keeps the vehicle aloft as it moves through the air. Lift acts on both the underside and upper side of an aircraft's wing's. On the upper side of a wing, lift is mainly in the form of suction. On the underside of a wing's surface, it performs as an upward, pushing action.

Mach number: A plane traveling faster than the speed of sound is said to be flying at supersonic speed. Supersonic speeds are rated according to mach numbers. Mach 1 is the speed of sound; mach 2 is twice that speed; mach 3 is three times the speed of sound, and so forth. The word comes from the name of an Austrian physicist, Ernst Mach, who devised the system of rating supersonic speeds.

Pod: This term is often used to identify that part of an aircraft's structure containing one or more airplane engines.

Ramjet: This is a type of jet engine with no moving parts. Air is rammed into the front end of the engine by the forward motion of the aircraft. The air is compressed and mixed with fuel in the burning chamber, and ignited. Superheated gases are produced that roar out of the tail of the engine, creating a powerful forward thrust. The ramjet engine is practical mainly for aircraft flying at supersonic speeds of mach 4 and higher.

Retrorockets: These are small rocket engines whose thrust is opposite to the flight path of the air or space vehicle on which they are used. Their main purpose is to help maneuver or slow the speed of a space vehicle.

Sonic boom: When an aircraft travels at the speed of sound or faster, shock waves form along the front portions of the body and wings. As the waves build up, they radiate from the moving airplane all the way to the earth below. When the waves reach ground level, they make a booming, thunderclap sound. Sonic booms have been known to shatter windows and crack the walls of houses.

Speed of sound: This is the speed at which sound waves travel through the air. It is commonly considered to be roughly 750 miles per hour. However, the speed varies according to such conditions as altitude, temperature, and humidity. Thus, it may range from the low 700's to about 750 miles per hour.

Thrust: This is the measure of power produced by a turbojet or rocket engine. The force with which an engine pushes against a structure to which it is attached is measured in terms of pounds of thrust. The amount of thrust is determined by placing the engine on a movable test stand, with a calibrated scale fixed to the stand. When the engine runs at full power and pushes against the stand, its thrust is measured precisely on the scale in pounds.

Vertical Stabilizer: This part of an airplane's tail section is sometimes called the vertical fin (as in this book). The vertical fin helps to stabilize an aircraft flying in a straight path. The aircraft's rudder is usually attached to the stabilizer. The rudder, of course, helps the pilot to steer the plane in right or left turning maneuvers.

Books for Further Reading

Barnaby, Captain Ralph S. *How To Make And Fly Paper Airplanes*. New York: Bantam Books, 1970. (paperback)

Mander, Jerry, George Dippel, and Howard Gossage. *The Great International Paper Airplane Book*. New York: Simon and Schuster, 1967.

Murray, William D. and Francis J. Rigney. *Paper Folding For Beginners*. New York: Dover Publications, Inc., 1960. (paperback)

Editors of *Year*. *A Pictorial History of Aviation*. New York: Year, Inc., 1961.

Index